FRED ZINNEMANN

INTERVIEWS

CONVERSATIONS WITH FILMMAKERS SERIES
PETER BRUNETTE, GENERAL EDITOR

Photo credit: Photofest

FRED ZINNEMANN

INTERVIEWS

EDITED BY GABRIEL MILLER

UNIVERSITY PRESS OF MISSISSIPPI / JACKSON

www.upress.state.ms.us

The University Press of Mississippi is a member of
the Association of American University Presses.

Copyright © 2005 by University Press of Mississippi

Manufactured in the United States of America

13 12 11 10 09 08 07 06 05   4 3 2 1

∞

Library of Congress Cataloging-in-Publication Data

Zinnemann, Fred, 1907–
    Fred Zinnemann : interviews / edited by Gabriel Miller.
      p. cm. — (Conversations with filmmakers series)
    Filmography: p.
    Includes index.
    ISBN 1-57806-697-2 (alk. paper) — ISBN 1-57806-698-0 (pbk. : alk. paper)
      1. Zinnemann, Fred, 1907– —Interviews. 2. Motion picture producers
and directors—United States—Interviews. I. Miller, Gabriel, 1948– II. Title.
III. Series.

PN1998.3.Z56A5 2005

                                                        2004052602

British Library Cataloging-in-Publication Data available

CONTENTS

INTRODUCTION

Fred Zinnemann's distinguished career as a filmmaker spanned fifty years, twenty-two feature films, eighteen short subjects, and a documentary. Zinnemann won four Academy Awards: one for a short subject (*That Mothers Might Live*, 1938), one for a documentary (*Benjy*, 1951), and two for feature films (*From Here to Eternity*, 1953; *A Man for All Seasons*, 1966). The Academy nominated him five more times for "Best Director" (*The Search*, 1948; *High Noon*, 1952; *The Nun's Story*, 1959; *The Sundowners*, 1960; and *Julia*, 1977). His direction was honored by the New York Film Critics four times and by the Directors Guild of America three times. In 1970 that later organization also awarded him the D. W. Griffith Award for lifetime achievement.

Although a product of the Hollywood studio system, Zinnemann was always a maverick, choosing his projects carefully and making films that reflected his cultural and philosophic aesthetic. His independent streak was demonstrated on his very first Hollywood job, as an extra on *All Quiet on the Western Front* (1930), when he was fired for talking back to the assistant director (see Phillips, Buckley, DeVeau). He was also the first director to be suspended from MGM after turning down directing assignments on three consecutive projects in 1947 (see Phillips, Buckley, DeVeau). In spite of these occasional run-ins with studio executives, Zinnemann still expressed affection and respect for the studio system. He admired its executives as showmen who had a feel and love for their product unlike the studio heads of more recent years, who he felt "don't know anything about show business" (American Film Institute;

see also Phillips). He also credited the studios with allowing fledgling directors to mature and learn their craft (see Buckley, Phillips).

Zinnemann's central formative experience was the year he spent with documentary filmmaker Robert Flaherty, with whom he went to Berlin in 1931 to work on a documentary about a nomadic tribe in central Asia. The film was never made, but Zinnemann learned much from the example of Flaherty, a fiercely independent artist, who confirmed for Zinnemann his already innate tendency to rely primarily on his own judgment and his belief in film artists' need to be as independent as possible from producers (see Neve, Buckley, American Film Institute, Phillips). Zinnemann told Gene Phillips and others that Flaherty "was the greatest single influence on my work as a filmmaker."

Working with Flaherty also solidified Zinnemann's predisposition for the documentary/realist style, the approach that marked his best work, especially *High Noon*, *From Here to Eternity*, and *The Nun's Story*. His first major film, *The Search* (1948), about displaced children in Europe after World War II, was the first film to be shot on location in Nuremburg, Munich, Frankfort, and Wurzbrug, and Zinnemann cast it with children who had actually been in concentration camps. Writing about the project in *Sight and Sound* (Autumn 1948), he emphasized this use of "the raw materials of history in order to make a dramatic document." The film garnered much critical praise, the *New York Times* calling it "a major revelation in our times," and it established Zinnemann's reputation.

The style later honed by Zinnemann in major studio films was apparent in his first feature, *Redes* (*The Wave*, 1934). Working under commission by the Mexican government, Zinnemann used the fishermen of the Gulf of Vera Cruz as nonprofessional actors to tell their own story. The film deals with the economic exploitation of the fishermen of a small village and the eventual killing of the protagonist who tries to organize his fellow workers.

This short film would also introduce the archetypal Zinnemann protagonist, a man of conscience who is compelled to confront the impersonal forces that threaten the freedom or livelihood of the individual and stand up for what he/she thinks is just. Zinnemann was fond of quoting the Jewish sage Hillel, "If I am not myself, who will be for me? And if I am only for myself, what am I? And if not now, when?" This became for the director his most significant thematic question (see Phillips).

Zinnemann said often that he finds "questions of conscience very pho-togenic" (American Film Institute). And the central conflicts in his films involve the individual against the community (*The Seventh Cross*, *High Noon*) or the individual's struggle to follow his/her conscience against enormous difficulties (*From Here to Eternity*, *The Nun's Story*, *Julia*, *The Member of the Wedding*) or a conflict that rages in the soul of the individual (*A Man for All Seasons*, *High Noon*). On another occasion he remarked, "I have always been concerned with the problem of the individual who struggles to preserve personal integrity and self-respect" (Buckley).

He also believed in making films that were positive and emphasized the innate dignity of human beings (see American Film Institute, Phillips, Nolletti). Zinnemann preferred stories that dealt with oppression, not necessarily political, but as he put it in a "human way" (see American Film Institute). In such circumstances the dramas he preferred could be played out. He realized his limitations as a director and recognized that there were certain kinds of films that he couldn't or shouldn't do. He admitted to a miscalculation in agreeing to film *Oklahoma!* (1955): "I tried to humanize it . . . I failed to bring *Oklahoma!* to the screen with the kind of purity it had on the stage" (Buckley; see also American Film Institute, Phillips, Gow, DeVeau).

Zinnemann's preoccupation with the oppression of human dignity and conscience and his commitment to make films that mattered are revealed in his extreme disappointment at the cancellation of his projected film of Andre Malraux's *Man's Fate*, which had consumed the better part of four years after the release of *A Man for All Seasons* in 1966. Zinnemann described the novel—which dealt with the repression of Chinese communists by Chiang Kai-shek in 1927—as a book "my generation worshipped" (Buckley). Zinnemann had what he considered an excellent script by Han Suyin and a cast that included Peter Finch, Max von Sydow, Liv Ullmann, and David Niven. The company had completed rehearsals, sets had been built, and after three years of preparation, the project was days away from beginning filming after over three years of preparation when James Aubrey, who had just taken over MGM, decided to cancel it as a cost-cutting measure. A lawsuit followed, but the experience "shattered" Zinnemann.

In discussing the kinds of stories and projects that interested him, Zinnemann was also quite adamant about the role of the director.

While skeptical about the auteur theory, which he labeled a "gimmick," he was insistent upon the primacy of the director—"the only man who had the central vision of the film." A strong director with vision was the one who integrated all the contributions of others into a whole that reflected *his* vision of the film. When the film was completed, it was "that man's picture" (Nolletti).

That being said, Zinnemann is consistently generous in the interviews collected here in acknowledging important contributions made by others. Most notable in this regard are his discussions of *High Noon*, surely one of his most famous and highly regarded works. He tells Michael Buckley that *High Noon* was actually "the work of four men" and in his interview with Gene Phillips he calls it a "team effort." He is unstinting in his praise for cinematographer Floyd Crosby, who managed to give the film the look of a newsreel. He also praises the contributions of writer Carl Foreman, editor Elmo Williams, and composer Dimitri Tiomkin (see Nolletti, Buckley, Phillips, Silke).

In these interviews, Zinnemann speaks with great affection and admiration for his actors and writers, emphasizing the contributions they made to his films. He is questioned most often about two actors whose screen careers he practically launched: Marlon Brando, who made his screen debut in *The Men*, and Montgomery Clift, whose first released film was *The Search*. (Technically his first film was *Red River*, but *The Search* was released first.) At Zinnemann's insistence, Clift would go on to appear in *From Here to Eternity* as well, although the studio wanted Aldo Ray, who was under contract. Meryl Streep (*Julia*); Pier Angeli, Ralph Meeker, and Rod Steiger (*Teresa*); and Jessica Tandy (*The Seventh Cross*) also made their film debuts under Zinnemann's direction. His actors won six Oscars (Gary Cooper, Paul Scofield, Frank Sinatra, Donna Reed, Vanessa Redgrave, and Jason Robards) and were nominated for numerous others.

Zinnemann's career was also distinguished by the variety of actors he worked with. He seemed equally at home with the Method actors who were beginning to break into film when his directing career was taking off, coaxing sensitive performances from Montgomery Clift, Marlon Brando, and Julie Harris, but he worked equally well with established stars like Burt Lancaster, Gregory Peck, Gary Cooper, Anthony Quinn, and Jane Fonda. He persuaded other actors to play against type, which resulted in two Oscar nominations for Deborah Kerr (*From Here to Eternity*, *The Sundowners*) and one for Audrey Hepburn (*The Nun's Story*).

Zinnemann was always sensitive in finding the particular film artists he felt would best serve a project. Thus he chose cinematographers Jean Badal, who shot the Hungarian Revolution, to provide the documentary flavor for *Behold a Pale Horse* and Jack Hilliard to achieve the romantic mood for *The Sundowners* (see Silke). He was just as determined to ensure that the screenplays reflected his vision, working with Carl Foreman on four films (uncredited on *A Hatful of Rain*), with the playwrights Robert Anderson and Robert Bolt, and with Isobel Lennart and Alvin Sargent.

Zinnemann was also a meticulous planner on his films, conducting enormous amounts of research on his films and preparing his own drawings of sequences and story boards—"because these things are so personal and so important to me that if the designer does them they look marvelous, but they're never quite what I want" (Silke). This hands-on dedication is surely one of the reasons that Zinnemann made relatively few features in forty years. The importance of preparation was part of his apprenticeship as a maker of shorts at MGM. In those days, promising directors usually worked their way up, and Zinnemann speaks favorably of his gradual ascent through the ranks. In one interview he explains his attitude which also reflects his European roots: "I go by the old idea of guilds, in which there are three stages. You are first an apprentice, then you become a journeyman, and if you are still in one piece, you eventually become what they call a master" (Neve).

At MGM, "apprentice" directors sometimes started on B films (intended for the second half of a theater's double bill) or, as was the case with Zinnemann, they were assigned to direct short subjects. Zinnemann directed eighteen of these between 1937 and 1941, most of them one- to two-reelers with an average shooting schedule of three days per reel. Having learned from Flaherty the value of researching a subject thoroughly before filming, however, Zinnemann was able to tell a wide variety of stories in these shorts, ranging in subject matter from biographies of George Washington Carver and Dr. Ephraim McDowell, the first doctor to perform surgery, to exposés of employment agencies and the tactics of foreign spies, to stories about the life of a submarine and the scourge of child-bed fever.

Zinnemann learned to tell these stories as economically as possible (see Phillips, Buckley, American Film Institute) while also maintaining a dramatic narrative line. His fondness for the documentary/realist approach pushed him to develop a style that is rich in the use of detail but carefully incorporates detail and setting within the mise en scène. Zinnemann's films are tightly structured while offering numerous sequences loaded with emotional and thematic imagery. *The Search* and *The Men* are early examples of his skill in applying a documentary approach to the portrayal of emotionally powerful stories.

Despite his thematic consistency, the symmetry and structural grace of his best work, the visual splendor of such films as *High Noon, The Sundowners, The Nun's Story,* and *Julia,* and the many awards bestowed on the man and his work, Zinnemann's films have generally been ignored by auteurist critics and others. The most popular disparagement of his work is that it is impersonal or too objective. J. R. Silke, for example, takes Zinnemann to task for not "taking sides," particularly in his presentation of characters (see also Neve, Nolletti).

Zinnemann was bothered by the decline in his critical reputation after he retired from directing in 1982, and he was not shy about confronting critics who he felt were misrepresenting or misunderstanding his work. This was certainly the case in his interview with Silke, who in a previous issue of *Cinema,* had berated Zinnemann for his "objectivism." Zinnemann's response reflects a position that he reiterated often: "It's a perfectly valid approach to present a problem or a question or an issue to an audience and let them determine for themselves how they feel about it." Throughout the interviews that follow, he takes pains in pointing out that he deliberately left the conclusion of *The Nun's Story* open-ended because he felt it wrong to influence the audience for or against the institution of religious life. He also believed this distance from the central character was one of the strengths of *High Noon.*

When confronted with Howard Hawks's objection to *High Noon,* that a sheriff in the Old West would not run around asking people for help as Will Kane does, Zinnemann always politely disagreed. He felt that his protagonist's actions were more consistent with *human* behavior, not *generic Western hero* behavior—indeed, Zinnemann never was comfortable talking about *High Noon* as a Western. "It seems to me that it's perfectly obvious that no one can tell ahead of time what the situation will be or how it will develop or whether he can cope with it all by himself."

Zinnemann did not believe in portraying heroes and heavies in his films, regarding that approach as too easy, too simplistic. Although he himself was involved and passionate about a variety of issues, his focus in his films was on the examination of character—how individuals reacted when faced with a difficult moral or political dilemma. Zinnemann's social-realist proclivities are evident in his attention to authentic settings, personalities, and detail. Social-realist filmmakers often display a reformist impulse, but although Zinnemann may cast a critical eye on societal problems, they do not form the narrative center of his films. Instead, his characters take center stage. Thus, two love stories subsume Zinnemann's sardonic take on military conformism in *From Here to Eternity*. The coming-of-age dilemmas of Frankie Addams eclipse racism in the undervalued *The Member of the Wedding*, where Zinnemann beautifully depicts the Addams home in all its tawdry detail while picking out symbolic images of psychological entrapment and suffocation. His ability to portray scenes realistically while also evoking a sense of otherness is most apparent in *The Nun's Story*, where his staging of religious rituals and pictures of Christian iconography achieves a spiritual luminosity that is unequaled elsewhere in film. (He manages to repeat this same sublime effect in some scenes of *A Man for All Seasons*.)

Zinnemann's films are thus difficult to categorize. His social-realist tendencies mix with his psychological focus. Zinnemann often concentrates on romantic involvements, but his films are decidedly unromantic. The social/economic problems of his characters often subvert love, either overtly, as in *From Here to Eternity*, *Teresa*, and *A Hatful of Rain* or more equivocally, as in *High Noon* and *Five Days One Summer*. Even in *Julia*, the relationship between Dashiell Hammett and Lillian Hellman, which was presented in legendary romantic terms by others, is downplayed by Zinnemann, who makes Lillian's relationship with Julia seem more tender than her relationship with Hammett.

Zinnemann's refusal to resort to either cut-and-dried political/social solutions or to standard romantic Hollywood endings is in part responsible for the all-too-easy labeling of his films as clinical or detached. In fact, neither of these dismissive labels is accurate, for Zinnemann explores each of his social landscapes as unique and seeks the same individuality in his characters. Zinnemann's protagonists bring their own perspectives to bear on the world they find themselves in and each defines him or herself accordingly. This, again, is why Zinnemann is fond of dramatizing conflicts of conscience, in which each character must strive to maintain his or her integrity in the face of restrictive pressures.

Zinnemann's devotion to this kind of character study is unusual in that he does not flinch from dramatizing the awful costs that these crises of conscience exact on his protagonists. Many of Zinnemann's characters are intelligent and articulate, and they are painfully aware of what their decisions will cost them. In *A Man for All Seasons*, for example, Zinnemann presents Thomas More as a man who has everything: wealth, prestige, power, a loving family, and a beautiful home. During the course of the film, however, he is gradually stripped of all of these blessings. Even Zinnemann's frame confines More ever more tightly as his options dwindle. He ultimately loses his life, as does the title character in *Julia* and Prewitt in *From Here to Eternity*, who like More, are painfully cognizant of the implications of their decisions.

Those films are reminders that Zinnemann's films often end on a bleak note. Even those that seem to promise "happy" endings (*The Men, High Noon, The Search, A Hatful of Rain*) are equivocal. This somber sensibility, however, is the ironic undertone of an essential humanism. Zinnemann had great sympathy for human beings and gloried in human aspiration and the accomplishment of human civilization. He endorsed, as he states in these interviews, William Faulkner's testament that the human race will "prevail." He was a great believer in romance (*The Sundowners, From Here to Eternity, A Man for All Seasons*), but he refused to pander to Hollywood excess. He was a great champion of idealism and the integrity of conscience, but he never shied away from confronting its awful price. His best films continue to be among the American cinema's most enduring accomplishments.

There is inevitably some repetition in this collection. Many of Zinnemann's views on matters regarding his films changed little over the years, and it is natural to find him repeating the same thoughts and stories about specific films and incidents from his life. As with all books in the Conversations with Filmmakers series, the interviews are reproduced unedited (except for some typographical errors and in some cases errors in fact) and in chronological order.

Finally, some thank-yous are in order. First to Barbara Hall of the Margaret Herrick Library, an exceptional reference librarian, who helped me in numerous ways. I would also like to thank Tim Zinnemann, who was generous in extending his permission to reprint his father's interviews and who sent me a copy of *As I See It*, a film tribute to his father that he produced and made with Walter Murch. Thank you to the editorial staff of the University Press of Mississippi, who were, as always, gracious and helpful. Thanks are due as well to all those who granted permission to make this material available. My most profound thank-you is, as always to Lizzie and Jessica, and especially to Kathy, for everything.

GM

CHRONOLOGY

1907	Born in Vienna on April 29 to Oskar Zinnemann, a prominent physician, and Anna Feiwel.
1927	Graduates from the University of Vienna with a degree in law.
1927–1928	Studies at the Technical School of Cinematography in Paris. While a student, contributes to Eugene Deslow's avant-garde documentary *La Marche des Machines* (1927).
1929	Moves to Berlin where he works as an assistant cameraman on two films, including *Menschen am Sonntag (People on Sunday)*, scripted by Billy Wilder and directed by Robert Siodmak. Comes to America and arrives in New York City on the day of the stock market crash; arrives in Hollywood with a letter of introduction to Carl Laemmle, head of Universal Studios.
1930	Laemmle gets him a job as an extra in *All Quiet on the Western Front* (Lewis Milestone) in which he doubles as German soldier and a French ambulance driver. He is fired after three weeks for talking back to the assistant director.
1930–1932	Hired by Fox as assistant to director Berthold Viertel. Also assists dance director Busby Berkeley on *The Kid from Spain* (Leo McCarey).
1931	Travels with Robert Flaherty to Berlin to plan a documentary about nomadic tribes in central Asia. The film was never made.

1934   Assistant to the costume designer and extra in *Nana*
          (Dorothy Arzner).
1935   Assistant director for *The Dark Angel* (Sidney Franklin)
          and *Peter Ibbetson* (Henry Hathaway). Directs his first
          feature film *Redes* (*The Wave*), filmed on location in the
          Gulf of Vera Cruz.
1936   Marries Renee Bartlett.
1937   Becomes an American citizen.
1938–1942 Directs eighteen shorts at MGM, contributing to several
          series: the Pete Smith Specialties, John Nesbitt's *Passing
          Parade*, and the Carey Wilson Miniatures. *That Mothers
          Might Live*, the story of a pioneer in the use of antiseptics
          in obstetrics, wins an Academy Award for Best Short
          Subject in 1938.
1940   Son Tim born.
1942   Directs his first two feature fiction films for MGM, both
          low-budget thrillers: *Kid Glove Killer* and *Eyes in the Night*.
1944   Directs his first A-list film, *The Seventh Cross*, starring
          Spencer Tracy.
1945   Assigned to direct Judy Garland in *The Clock* but is
          replaced by Vincente Minnelli, who married Garland
          that year.
1947   Directs two Jackie "Butch" Jenkins vehicles, *My Brother
          Talks to Horses* and *Little Mister Jim*. Declines his next
          three assignments and becomes the first director in MGM
          history to be suspended.
1948   Directs *The Search* (*Die Gezeichneten*) in Europe, starring
          Montgomery Clift. The film is nominated for an Academy
          Award as Best Picture and Zinnemann is nominated as
          Best Director. Directs *Act of Violence*, starring Robert Ryan,
          Van Heflin, and Mary Astor.
1949   Signs a three-picture deal with independent producer
          Stanley Kramer.
1950   Directs *The Men*, starring Marlon Brando in his film debut.
1951   Returns to MGM for *Teresa*, starring Pier Angeli in her
          screen debut. Film also features the debuts of Rod Steiger
          and Ralph Meeker. Stewart Stern's screenplay is nominated

for an Academy Award. *Benjy*, a fund-raising short (also scripted by Stern) made for the Orthopedic Hospital of Los Angeles, wins the Academy Award for Best Documentary.

1952   Directs *High Noon*, starring Gary Cooper (Oscar winner). Both Zinnemann and the film are nominated for Academy Awards. The New York Film Critics honor both the film and Zinnemann as Best Director. Directs *The Member of the Wedding*, his last film for Stanley Kramer, starring Julie Harris (Oscar nomination) and Ethel Waters.

1953   Directs *From Here to Eternity*, his most honored film, which wins eight out of thirteen Academy Award nominations. Both Zinnemann and the film win Academy Awards and New York Film Critics Awards. Zinnemann also wins the Directors Guild Award.

1955   Directs *Oklahoma!* first film made in Wide Screen Todd-AO. Shirley Jones stars in her screen debut opposite Gordon MacRae.

1956   Begins filming Hemingway's *The Old Man and the Sea*. Quits the film because of difficulties with Spencer Tracy. He is replaced by John Sturges.

1957   Directs *A Hatful of Rain*, starring Don Murray, Anthony Franciosa (Oscar nomination), and Eva Marie Saint.

1959   Directs *The Nun's Story*, starring Audrey Hepburn. Film is nominated for eight Academy Awards, including Best Picture, Best Actress, and Best Director. Wins his third Best Director award from the New York Film Critics.

1960   Directs *The Sundowners*, starring Robert Mitchum, Deborah Kerr, and Peter Ustinov. Film is nominated for five Academy Awards, including Best Picture, Best Actress, and Best Director.

1961–1963   Works on *Hawaii*, which he abandons for lack of a workable script. Supervises *Exercise No. One* (a.k.a *Off the Highway*), a film made by the Student Industry Film Group in association with the University of Southern California.

1964   Directs *Behold a Pale Horse*, starring Gregory Peck, Anthony Quinn, and Omar Sharif.

1966   Directs *A Man for All Seasons*, starring Paul Scofield,
                Wendy Hiller, Susannah York, Robert Shaw, and Orson
                Welles. Film wins six Academy Awards, including Best
                Picture, Best Actor, and Best Director. Wins fourth New
                York Film Critics Award as Best Director.

1969–1970   Works on *Man's Fate*, based on the novel by
                André Malraux. With a finished script and a cast (Peter
                Finch, David Niven, Liv Ullmann, and Max von Sydow)
                Zinnemann is ready to begin filming when the produc-
                tion is abruptly canceled by MGM. He sues. Wins the
                D. W. Griffith Award for Lifetime Achievement from the
                Directors Guild.

1973   Directs *The Day of the Jackal*, starring Edward Fox.

1974   Prepares film *Abelard and Heloise*, which does not
                get made.

1977   Directs *Julia*, starring Jane Fonda and Vanessa Redgrave
                (Oscar winner). Film is nominated for eleven Academy
                Awards, including Best Picture and Best Director.

1982   Directs *Five Days One Summer*, his last film, starring Sean
                Connery. Retrospective of his films at London's National
                Film Theatre.

1983   Retrospective honoring his career at Cinémathèque
                Française.

1988   Career retrospective at the University of Southern
                California.

1994   Receives the John Huston Award for Artists Rights.

1996   Receives Lifetime Achievement Award at the Berlin Film
                Festival.

1997   March 14, dies in London.

FILMOGRAPHY

Short Films

1938
A FRIEND IN DEED (A Pete Smith Specialty), screenplay by Barney Gerard, music by William Axt

THE STORY OF DR. CARVER, screenplay by Robert Lees and Fred Rinaldo, photography by Robert Pittack, music by William Axt

THAT MOTHERS MIGHT LIVE, screenplay by Herman Boxer, narrated by John Nesbitt, photography by Harold Rosson, music by David Snell

TRACKING THE SLEEPING DEATH, original story and screenplay by Richard Goldstone, narrated by Carey Wilsoe, music by David Snell

THEY LIVE AGAIN, screenplay by Herman Boxer, narrated by John Nesbitt, music by David Snell

1939
WEATHER WIZARDS (A Pete Smith Specialty), screenplay by Robert Lees and Fred Rinaldo, narrated by Pete Smith

WHILE AMERICA SLEEPS (A Crime Does Not Pay Subject), original story and screenplay by Karl Kamb, photography by Paul Vogel, edited by Ralph E. Goldstein

HELP WANTED! (A Crime Does Not Pay Subject), story by Elizabeth Shaw, screenplay by Winston Miller and Karl Kamb, edited by Ralph E. Goldstein

ONE AGAINST THE WORLD (John Nesbitt's *Passing Parade*), story by Barney Gerard, screenplay by Doane Hoag, edited by Albert Akst, music by C. Bakaleinikoff

THE ASH CAN FLEET, original story and screenplay by Herman Hoffman, photography by Paul Vogel, edited by Harry Komer, music by C. Bakaleinikoff and D. Amfitheatrof

FORGOTTEN VICTORY (John Nesbitt's *Passing Parade*), screenplay by Robert Lopez, narrated by John Nesbitt, photography by Harold Rosson, edited by Harry Komer, music by D. Amfitheatrof

1940
THE OLD SOUTH, screenplay by Herman Hoffman, photography by Jackson Rose, edited by Roy Brickner, music by D. Amfitheatrof

STUFFIE (A Pete Smith Specialty), screenplay and narration by Pete Smith, edited by Philip Anderson, music by David Snell

A WAY IN THE WILDERNESS (John Nesbitt's *Passing Parade*), screenplay by Herman Boxer, narrated by John Nesbitt, photography by Paul Vogel, art direction by Richard Duce, edited by Albert Akst, music by David Snell

THE GREAT MEDDLER (A Carey Wilson Miniature), story by Joseph Ansen, screenplay by Julian Hochfelder and Barney Gerard

1941
FORBIDDEN PASSAGE (A Crime Does Not Pay Subject), screenplay by Carl Dudley, photography by Jackson Rose, art direction by Richard Duce, edited by Albert Akst

YOUR LAST ACT (John Nesbitt's *Passing Parade*), screenplay by Doane Hoag, based on an idea by Norman Rose, narrated by John Nesbitt, photography by Harold Lipstein, art direction by Richard Duce, edited by Albert Akst, music by Lennie Hayton

1942
THE LADY OR THE TIGER? (A Carey Wilson Miniature), screenplay by Herman Boxer, based on the story by Frank R. Stockton, edited by Adrienne Fazan

1951
BENJY, screenplay by Stewart Stern, narrated by Henry Fonda, photography by J. Peverell Marley, edited by George Tomasini, with Lee Aaker, Marille Phelps, Adam Williams, and Neville Brand; produced by the Orthopaedic Foundation of Los Angeles; 30 minutes

Feature Films

1934
THE WAVE (REDES OR PESCADOS)
Mexican Federal Department of Fine Arts
Producer: Paul Strand
Director: **Zinnemann** (Note: There are sources that credit Emilio Gómez Muriel as co-director. **Zinnemann** disputed this.)
Screenplay: Henwar Rodakiewicz, Emilio Gómez Muriel, **Zinnemann**
Photography: Paul Strand
Editing: Gunther Von Fritsch and Emilio Gómez Muriel
Music: Sylvestre Revueltas
Cast: Silvio Hernández (Miro, the young fisherman), David Valle González, Rafael Hinojosa, Antonio Lara, Miguel Figueroa, and the people of Alvarado
Black and White
60 minutes

1942
KID GLOVE KILLER
MGM

Producer: Jack Chertok
Director: **Zinnemann**
Screenplay: Allen Rivken and John C. Higgins (story by Higgins)
Photography: Paul Vogel
Art Direction: Randall Duell and Cedric Gibbons
Editing: Ralph Winters
Music: David Snell
Cast: Van Heflin (Gordon McKay), Marsha Hunt (Jane Mitchell), Lee Bowman (Gerald I. Ladimer), Samuel S. Hinds (Mayor Daniels), Cliff Clark (Captain Lynch), Eddie Quillan (Eddie Wright), Ava Gardner (car-hop waitress), John Litel (Matty), Catherine Lewis (Bessie Wright), and Nella Walker (Mrs. Daniels)
Black and white
74 minutes

EYES IN THE NIGHT
MGM
Producer: Jack Chertok
Director: **Zinnemann**
Screenplay: Guy Trosper and Howard Emmett Rogers (based on the novel *Odor of Violets* by Baynard Kendrick)
Photography: Robert Planck and Charles Lawton
Art Direction: Cedric Gibbons and Stan Rogers
Editing: Ralph Winters
Music: Lennie Hayton
Cast: Edward Arnold (Duncan Maclain), Ann Harding (Norma Lawry), Donna Reed (Barbara Lawry), Allen Jenkins (Marty), John Emery (Paul Gerente), Horace [Stephen] McNally (Gabriel Hoffman), Katherine Emery (Cheli Scott), Rosemary DeCamp (Vera Hoffman), Stanley C. Ridges (Hansen), Reginald Denny (Stephen Lawry), Barry Nelson (Busch), Steve Geray (Anderson), Erik Rolf (Boyd), Reginald Sheffield (Victor), Ivan Miller (Herman), Milburn Stone (Pete), Mantan Moreland (Alistair), Cliff Danielson (boy), Frances Rafferty (girl), Edward Kilroy (pilot), John Butler (driver), William Nye (Hugo), Frank Thomas (police lieutenant), Marie Windsor (actress), and "Friday" (Alsatian)
B & W
79 minutes

1944
THE SEVENTH CROSS
MGM
Producer: Pandro S. Berman
Director: **Zinnemann**
Screenplay: Helen Deutsch (from the novel by Anna Seghers)
Photography: Karl Freund (uncredited additional photography by Robert Surtees)
Art Direction: Cedric Gibbons and Leonid Vasian
Editing: Thomas Richards
Music: Roy Webb
Cast: Spencer Tracy (George Heisler), Signe Hasso (Toni), Hume Cronyn (Paul Roeder), Jessica Tandy (Liesel Roeder), Agnes Moorehead (Madame Marelli), Ray Collins (Ernest Wallau; the film's narrator), Herbert Rudley (Franz Marnet), Felix Bressart (Poldi Schlamm), George Macready (Bruno Sauer), Katherine Locke (Mrs. Sauer), Steven Geray (Dr. Loewenstein), Paul Guilfoyle (Fiedler), Kurt Katch (Leo Hermann), Alexander Granach (Zillich), Karen Verne (Leni), Konstantin Shayne (Fuellgrabe), George Suzanne (Bellani), John Wengraf (Overkamp), George Zucco (Fahrenburg), Steven Muller (Hellwig), Eily Malyon (Fräulein Bachmann), Paul E. Burns (Pelzer), Hugh Beaumont (truck driver), William Tannen (guard), William Challee (Fischer), and Ludwig Donath (Wilhelm Reinhardt)
B & W
112 minutes

1947
MY BROTHER TALKS TO HORSES
MGM
Producer: Samuel Marx
Director: **Zinnemann**
Screenplay: Morton Thompson, from his story, "Lewie, My Brother Who Talks to Horses"
Photography: Harold Rosson
Art Direction: Cedric Gibbons and Leonid Vasian
Editing: George White

Music: Rudolph G. Kopp
Cast: Jackie "Butch" Jenkins (Lewie Penrose), Peter Lawford (John
S. Penrose), Beverly Tyler (Martha), Edward Arnold (Mr. Bledsoe),
Charles Ruggles (Richard Pennington Roeder), Spring Byington
(Mrs. Penrose), O. Z. Whitehead (Mr. Puddy), Paul Langton
(Mr. Gillespie), Ernest Whitman (Mr. Mordecai), Irving Bacon
(Mr. Piper), Lillian Yarbo (Psyche), Howard Freeman (Hector Damson),
and Harry Hayden (Mr. Gibley)
B & W
93 minutes

LITTLE MISTER JIM
MGM
Producer: Orville O. Dull
Director: **Zinnemann**
Screenplay: George Bruce, from the novel *The Army Brat* by Tommy
Wadelton
Photography: Lester White
Art Direction: Cedric Gibbons
Editing: Frank E. Hull
Music: George Bassman
Cast: Jackie "Butch" Jenkins (Little Jim Tukker), Frances Gifford
(Mrs. Tukker), James Craig (Big Jim Tukker), Luana Patten (Missy
Choosey), Ching Wah Lee (Sui Jen), Laura La Plante (Mrs. Glenson),
Spring Byington (Mrs. Starwell), Henry O'Neill (chaplain), Morris
Ankrum (Col. Starwell), Celia Travers (Miss Martin), Ruth Brady (Miss
Hall), Sharon McManus (Elsie McBride), Buz Buckley (Ronnie Shelton),
Carol Nugent (Clara), and Jean Van (Mary)
B & W
92 minutes

1948
THE SEARCH (DIE GEZEICHNETEN)
Praesens Film. Swiss and MGM release
Producer: Lazar Wechsler
Director: **Zinnemann**

Screenplay: Richard Schweizer and David Wechsler (additional dialogue
Paul Jarrico and [uncredited] Montgomery Clift)
Photography: Emil Berna
Editing: Hermann Haller
Music: Robert Blum
Cast: Montgomery Clift (Ralph "Steve" Stevenson), Aline MacMahon
(Mrs. Murray), Wendell Corey (Jerry Fisher), Jarmila Novotna
(Mrs. Malik), Ivan Jandl (Karel Malik), Mary Patton (Mrs. Fisher), Ewart G.
Morrison (Mr. Crookes), William Rogers (Tom Fisher), Leopold
Borkowski (Joel Markowsky), and Claude Gambier (Raoul Dubois)
B & W
105 minutes

1949
ACT OF VIOLENCE
MGM
Producer: William H. Wright
Director: **Zinnemann**
Screenplay: Robert L. Richards (story by Collier Young)
Photography: Robert Surtees
Art Direction: Cedric Gibbons and Hans Peters
Editing: Conrad A. Nervig
Music: Bronislau Kaper
Cast: Van Heflin (Frank Enley), Robert Ryan (Joe Parkson), Janet Leigh
(Edith Enley), Mary Astor (Pat), Phyllis Thaxter (Ann Sturges), Berry
Kroeger (Johnny), Taylor Holmes (Gavery), Harry Antrim (Fred Finney),
Connie Gilchrist (Martha Finney), Will Wright (boat rental man), John
Albright (bellboy), William Bailey (drunk at party), Bill Cartledge
(newsboy), Jim Drum (policeman), Phil Dunham (drunk at party), Dick
Elliott (drunk at party), Everett Glass (hotel night clerk), Don Haggerty
(policeman), Mahlon Hamilton (wino), Larry and Leslie Holt (Georgie
Enley), Wesley Hopper (policeman), Paul Kruger (policeman), Wilbur
Mack (drunk at party), Howard M. Mitchell (bartender), Roger Moore
(wino), Garry Owen (auto rental attendent), Ralph Peters (Tim the bartender), Fred Santley (drunk at party), Frank J. Scannell (bell captain),
Dick Simmons (veteran), Robert Skelton (cab driver), Phil Tead (hotel
day clerk), Candy Toxton (veteran's wife), and Eddie Waglin (bellboy)

B & W
85 minutes

1950
THE MEN (reissued in 1957 as BATTLE STRIPE)
United Artists
Producer: Stanley Kramer
Director: **Zinnemann**
Screenplay: Carl Foreman
Photography: Robert de Grasse
Production Design: Rudolph Sternad
Editing: Harry Gerstad
Music: Dimitri Tiomkin
Cast: Marlon Brando (Ken "Bud" Wilcheck), Teresa Wright (Ellen),
Everett Sloane (Dr. Eugene Brock), Jack Webb (Norm Butler), Richard
Erdman (Leo Doolin), Arthur Jurado (Angel Lopez), Virginia Farmer
(Nurse Robbins), Ray Teal (man in bar), Dorothy Tree (Harriet, Ellen's
mother), Howard St. John (Ellen's father), Nita Hunter (Dolores Lopez),
Patricia Joiner (Laverne), John Miller (Mr. Doolin), Cliff Clark
(Dr. Kameran), Marguerite Martin (Angel's mother), Virginia Christine
(patient's wife), Obie Parker (the lookout), Paul Peltz (Hopkins),
William Lea, Jr. (Walter), Tom Gillick (Fine), Ray Mitchell (Thompson),
Pete Simon (Mullin), Randall Updyke III (Baker), Marshall Ball
(Romano), Carlo Lewis (Gunderson), Ted Anderson (PVA board), Ralph
Brooks (therapist), Sayre Dearing (bar patron), Pat Grissom (PVA board),
Sherry Hall (bartender), John Hamilton (justice of the peace), Victoria
Home (paraplegic's wife), DeForest Kelley (Dr. Sherman), Mike Lally
(diner), William H. O'Brien (nightclub waiter), and Frank O'Connor
(orderly)
B & W
85 minutes

1951
TERESA
MGM
Producer: Arthur M. Loew, Jr.

Director: **Zinnemann**

Screenplay: Stewart Stern (from the novel *The Girl on the Via Flamina* by Alfred Hayes)

Photography: William J. Miller

Art Direction: Leo Kerz

Editing: Frank Sullivan and David Kummins

Music: Louis Applebaum

Cast: John Ericson (Philip Cass), Pier Angeli (Teresa), Patricia Collinge (Philip's mother), Ralph Meeker (Sgt. Dobbs), Richard Bishop (Philip's father), Rod Steiger (the army psychiatrist), Peggy Ann Garner (Susan), Edward Binns (Sgt. Brown), Bill Mauldin (Grissom, Philip's army friend), Ave Ninchi (Teresa's mother), Aldo Silvani (Teresa's father), Franco Interlenghi (Mario, Teresa's brother), Tommy Lewis (Walter), Edith Atwater (Mrs. Lawrence), Lewis Cianelli (Cheyenne), William King, Richard MacNamara, and Guido Marrudi

B & W

105 minutes

1952

HIGH NOON

Producer: Stanley Kramer

Director: **Zinnemann**

Screenplay: Carl Foreman, from the story "The Tin Star" by John W. Cunningham

Photography: Floyd Crosby

Production Design: Rudolph Sternad

Art Direction: Ben Hayne

Editing: Elmo Williams and Harry Gerstad

Music: Dimitri Tiomkin; song, "Do Not Forsake Me, Oh My Darlin'," by Tiomkin and Ned Washington, sung by Tex Ritter

Cast: Gary Cooper (Will Kane), Thomas Mitchell (Jonas Henderson), Lloyd Bridges (Harvey Pell), Katy Jurado (Helen Ramirez), Grace Kelly (Amy Kane), Otto Kruger (Judge Percy Mettrick), Lon Chaney, Jr. (Martin Howe, the former marshal), Ian MacDonald (Frank Miller), Howland Chamberlain (hotel clerk), Jack Elam (Charlie, the town drunk), Henry [Harry] Morgan (Sam Fuller), Eve McVeagh (Mildred

Fuller), Harry Shannon (Cooper), Lee Van Cleef (Jack Colby), Robert
Wilke (James Pierce), Sheb Wooley (Ben Miller), Tom London (Sam),
Ted Stanhope (station master), Larry Blake (Gillis), William Phillips
(barber), Morgan Farley (Dr. Mahin, minister), Guy Beach (Fred, the
coffin maker), Jeanne Blackford (Mrs. Henderson), Virginia Christine
(Mrs. Simpson), Cliff Clark (Ed Weaver), John Doucette (Trumbull),
Paul Dubov (Scott), Dick Elliott (Kibbee), Virginia Farmer
(Mrs. Fletcher), Tim Graham (Sawyer), Tom Greenway (Ezra), Harry
Harvey (Coy), Nolan Leary (Lewis), James Millican (Deputy Sheriff
Herb Baker), William Newell (Jimmy), Lucien Prival (Joe), Ralph Reed
(Johnny)
B & W
85 minutes

THE MEMBER OF THE WEDDING
Columbia
Producer: Stanley Kramer
Director: **Zinnemann**
Screenplay: Edward Anhalt and Edna Anhalt (from the Carson
McCullers play)
Photography: Hal Mohr
Production Design: Rudolph Sternad
Art Direction: Cary Odell
Editing: William A. Lyon
Music: Alex North
Cast: Julie Harris (Frankie Addams), Ethel Waters (Bernice Sadie Brown),
Brandon de Wilde (John Henry), Arthur Franz (Jarvis, Frankie's brother),
Nancy Gates (Janice), William Hansen (Mr. Addams, Frankie's brother),
James Edwards (Honey Camden Brown), Harry Bolden (T. T. Williams),
Dickie Moore (drunk soldier), Hugh Beaumont (minister), Danny
Mummert (Barney McKean), June Hedin (Helen), Ann Carter (Doris),
Charlcie Garrett, and Harry Richards
B & W
91 minutes

1953
FROM HERE TO ETERNITY

Columbia
Producer: Buddy Adler
Director: **Zinnemann**
Screenplay: Daniel Taradash (from the novel by James Jones)
Photography: Burnett Guffey and Floyd Crosby
Art Direction: Cary Odell
Editing: William A. Lyon
Music: George Duning
Cast: Burt Lancaster (Sgt. Milton Warden), Montgomery Clift (Pvt. Robert E. Lee "Prew" Prewitt), Deborah Kerr (Karen Holmes), Donna Reed (Alma "Lorene" Burke), Frank Sinatra (Pvt. Angelo Maggio), Philip Ober (Capt. Dana Holmes), Ernest Borgnine (Sgt. "Fatso" Judson), Mickey Shaughnessy (Sgt. Leva), Jack Warden (Cpl. Buckley), John Dennis (Sgt. Ike Galovich), Merle Tavis (Sal Anderson), Tim Ryan (Sgt. Pete Karelsen), Arthur Keegan (Treadwell), Barbara Morrison (Mrs. Kipfer), Jean Willes (Annette), George Reeves (Sgt. Maylon Stark), Harry Bellaver (Pvt. Mazzioli), Douglas Henderson (Cpl. Champ Wilson), Don Dubbins (Pvt. Friday Clark), Claude Akins (Sgt. Dhom), Robert Wilke (Sgt. Henderson), John Cason (Cpl. Paluso), Kristine Miller (Georgette), John Byrant (Capt. G. R. Ross), Joan Shawlee (Sandra), Angela Stevens (Jean), Mary Carver (Nancy), Vicki Bakken (Suzanne), Margaret Barstow (Roxanne), Delia Shavi (Billie), Willis Bouchey (lieutenant colonel), Alvin Sargent (Nair), William Lundmark (Bill), Weaver Levy (bartender), Tyler McVey (Maj. Stern), Moana Gleason (Rose), Robert Karnes (Sgt. Turp Thornhill), Manny Klein (trumpet player), Freeman Lusk (Col. Wood), Robert Pike (Maj. Bonds), Fay Roope (Gen. Slater), Jean Willes (Annette), and Carleton Young (Col. Ayres)
B & W
118 minutes

1955
OKLAHOMA!
Magna Theatre Corporation, Twentieth-Century Fox
Producer: Arthur Hornblow, Jr.
Executive Producers: Richard Rodgers and Oscar Hammerstein II

Director: **Zinnemann**
Screenplay: Sonya Levien and William Ludwig (adaption of musical play by Richard Rodgers and Oscar Hammerstein II, based on the play *Green Grow the Lilacs* by Lynn Riggs)
Photography: Robert Surtees and Floyd Crosby
Production Design: Oliver Smith
Art Direction: Joseph C. Wright
Editing: Gene Ruggiero and George Boemler
Choreography: Agnes De Mille
Music: Richard Rodgers and Adolph Deutsch; lyrics by Oscar Hammerstein II; conducted by Jay Blackton
Cast: Gordon MacRae (Curly McLain), Shirley Jones (Laurey Williams), Gloria Grahame (Ado Annie Carnes), Gene Nelson (Will Parker), Rod Steiger (Jud Fry), Charlotte Greenwood (Aunt Eller), James Whitmore (Judge Andrew Carnes), Eddie Albert (Ali Hakim, the Persian peddler), Barbara Lawrence (Gertie Cummings), Jay C. Flippen (Skidmore), James Mitchell (Curly in the Dream Ballet), Bambi Linn (Laurey in the Dream Ballet), Roy Barcroft (Marshal Cord Elam), Ben Johnson (wrangler), Donald Kerr (farmer), Russell Simpson (minister), and Rory Mallinson, Al Ferguson, and Buddy Roosevelt (cowboys at auction); dancers: Jennie Worksman, Marc Platt, Kelly Brown, Lizanne Truex, Jane Fischer, Virginia Bosler, Evelyn Taylor, Jerry Dealey, and Nancy Kilgas
Color
145 minutes

1957
A HATFUL OF RAIN
Twentieth-Century Fox
Producer: Buddy Adler
Director: **Zinnemann**
Screenplay: Michael Vincente Gazzo, Alfred Hayes and (uncredited) Carl Foreman from Gazzo's play
Photography: Joe MacDonald
Art Direction: Leland Fuller and Lyle R. Wheeler
Editing: Dorothy Spencer
Music: Bernard Herrmann

Cast: Eva Marie Saint (Celia Pope), Don Murray (Johnny Pope, Jr.), Anthony Franciosa (Polo Pope), Lloyd Nolan (John Pope, Sr.), Henry Silva ("Mother"), Gerald O'Loughlin (Church), William Hickey (Apples), William Tannen (executive), Michael Vale (cab driver), Art Fleming (mounted cop), Tom Ahearne (bartender), Norman Willis (John), Paul Kruger (bartender), Jason Johnson (boss), Emerson Treacy (office manager), Jay Jostyn (doctor), William Bailey, Gordon B. Clark, Rex Lease, Ralph Montgomery, and Herb Virgran

B & W

109 minutes

1959

THE NUN'S STORY

Warner Brothers

Producer: Henry Blanke

Director: **Zinnemann**

Screenplay: Robert Anderson, from the novel by Kathryn C. Hulme

Photography: Franz Planer

Art Direction: Alexandre Trauner

Editing: Walter Thompson

Music: Franz Waxman

Cast: Audrey Hepburn (Gabrielle van der Mal/Sister Luke), Peter Finch (Dr. Fortunati), Dame Edith Evans (Mother Emmanuel), Dame Peggy Ashcroft (Mother Mathilde), Dean Jagger (Dr. Hubert van der Mal), Mildred Dunnock (Sister Margharita, Mistress of Postulants), Beatrice Straight (Mother Christophe), Patricia Collinge (Sister William), Rosalie Crutchley (Sister Eleanor, Mistress of Novices), Patricia Bosworth (Simone/Sister Christine), Niall MacGinnis (Father Vermeuhlen), Colleen Dewhurst (Archangel Gabrielle, a schizophrenic patient), Dorothy Alison (Sister Aurelie), Ruth White (Mother Marcella), Eva Kotthaus (Sister Marie), Barbara O'Neil (Mother Katherine), Lionel Jeffries (Dr. Goovaerts), Margaret Phillips (Sister Pauline), Molly Urquhart (Sister Augustine), Stephen Murray (Chaplain), Orlando Martins (Kalulu), Errol John (Illunga), Jeanette Sterke (Louise), Richard O'Sullivan (Pierre), Diana Lambert (Lisa), Marina Wolkonsky (Marie), Penelope Horner (Jeannette Miloner), Ave Ninchi (Sister Bernard),

Charles Lamb (Pascini), Ludovince Bonhomme (Bishop), Dara Gavin
(Sister Ellen), and Elfrida Simbari (Sister Timothy)
Color
149 minutes

1960
THE SUNDOWNERS
Warner Bros.
Producer: Gerry Blatner
Director: **Zinnemann**
Screenplay: Isobel Lennart, from the novel by Jon Cleary
Photography: Jack Hildyard
Art Direction: Michael Stringer
Editing: Jack Harris
Music: Dimitri Tiomkin
Cast: Deborah Kerr (Ida Carmody), Robert Mitchum (Paddy Carmody),
Peter Ustinov (Rupert Venneker), Glynis Johns (Mrs. Gert Firth), Dina
Merrill (Jean Halstead), Chips Rafferty (Quinlan), Michael Anderson,
Jr. (Sean), Lola Brooks (Liz), Wylie Watson (Herb Johnson), John
Meillon (Bluey), Ronald Fraser (Ocker), Mervyn Johns (Jack Patchogue),
Molly Urquhart (Mrs. Bateman), Ewen Solon (Halstead), Dick Bentley
(shearer), Gerry Duggan (shearer), Peter Carver (shearer), Leonard Teale
(shearer), Alastair Williamson (shearer), Ray Barrett, and Mercia Barden
Color
133 minutes

1964
BEHOLD A PALE HORSE
Highland-Brentwood/Columbia
Producer: **Zinnemann**
Director: **Zinnemann**
Screenplay: J. P. Miller, from the novel *Killing a Mouse on Sunday* by
Emeric Pressburger
Photography: Jean Badal
Production Design: Alexandre Trauner
Art Direction: Auguste Capelier

Editing: Walter Thompson

Music: Maurice Jarre

Cast: Gregory Peck (Manuel Artiguez), Anthony Quinn (Capt. Viñolas), Omar Sharif (Father Francisco), Mildred Dunnock (Pilar), Raymond Pellegrin (Carlos, the informer), Paola Stoppa (Pedro), Daniela Rocca (Rosana, Viñolas' mistress), Rosalie Crutchley (Teresa, Viñolas' wife), Marietto Angeletti (Paco Dages), Christian Marquand (Zaganar, Viñolas' lieutenant), Michael Lonsdale (news reporter), Molly Urquhart (nurse), Perrette Pradier (Maria), Zia Mohyeddin (Luis), Jean-Paul Moulinot (Father Estiban), Laurence Badie (Celestina), Alain Saury (Lt. Sanchez), Martin Benson (priest), José Luis de Villallonga (horse dealer), Elisabeth Wiener (café girl), Jean- Claude Bercq, Claude Berri, and Claude Confortès

B & W

113 minutes

1966

A MAN FOR ALL SEASONS

Highland/Columbia Pictures

Producer: **Zinnemann** and William N. Graf

Director: **Zinnemann**

Screenplay: Robert Bolt, based on his play

Photography: Ted Moore

Production Design: John Box

Art Direction: Terence Marsh

Editing: Ralph Kemplen

Music: Georges Delerue

Cast: Paul Scofield (Sir Thomas More), Wendy Hiller (Lady Alice More), Leo McKern (Thomas Cromwell), Robert Shaw (King Henry VIII), Orson Welles (Cardinal Wolsey), Susannah York (Margaret More), Nigel Davenport (Duke of Norfolk), John Hurt (Richard Rich), Corin Redgrave (William Roper), Colin Blakely (Matthew), Vanessa Redgrave (Anne Boleyn), Cyril Luckham (Archbishop Cranmer), Jack Gwillim (chief justice), Thomas Heathcote (boatman), Yootha Joyce (Averil Machin), Anthony Nicholls (king's representative), John Nettleton (jailer), Eira Heath (Matthew's wife), Molly Urquhart (maid), Paul

Hardwick (courtier), Michael Latimer (Norfolk's aide), Philip Brack
(captain of guard), Martin Boddey (governor of tower), Eric Mason
(executioner), and Matt Zimmerman (messenger)
Color
120 minutes

1973
THE DAY OF THE JACKAL
Universal Studios
Producer: John Woolf, David Deutsch, and Julian Derode
Director: **Zinnemann**
Screenplay: Kenneth Ross, from novel by Frederick Forsyth
Photography: Jean Tournier
Production Design: Willy Holt and Ernest Archer
Editing: Ralph Kemplen
Music: Georges Delerue
Cast: Edward Fox ("The Jackal"), Michael Lonsdale (Chief Inspector
Claude Lebel), Delphine Seyrig (Colette de Montpelier), Terence
Alexander (Lloyd), Michel Auclair (Col. Rolland), Eric Porter (Col. Rodin),
Jean Martin (Wolenski), Denis Carey (Casson), Olga Georges-Picot
(Denise), Cyril Cusack (Gozzi, the gunsmith), Alan Badel (the minister),
Maurice Denham (Gen. Colbert), Donald Sinden (Mallinson), Tony
Britton (Inspector Thomas), Derek Jacobi (Caron, Lebel's assistant),
Adrien Cayla-Legrand (de Gaulle), Ronald Pickup (forger/blackmailer),
Vernon Dobtcheff (interrogator), Timothy West (Berthier), Jean Sorel
(Lt. Col. Bastien-Thiry), Barrie Ingham (St. Clair), Anton Rodgers
(Bernard), David Swift (Montclair), Bernard Archard (English detective),
Jacques François (Pascal), and Raymond Gérôme (Flavigny)
Color
142 minutes

1977
JULIA
Producer: Richard Roth
Director: **Zinnemann**
Screenplay: Alvin Sargent, from the story by Lillian Hellman in *Pentimento*

Photography: Douglas Slocombe
Production Design: Gene Callahan, Willy Holt, and Carmen Dillon
Editing: Marcel Durham and Walter Murch
Music: Georges Delerue
Cast: Jane Fonda (Lillian Hellman), Vanessa Redgrave (Julia), Jason
Robards, Jr. (Dashiell Hammett), Maximilian Schell (Johann), Hal
Holbrook (Alan Campbell), Rosemary Murphy (Dorothy Parker), Meryl
Streep (Anne Marie), Dora Doll (woman train passenger), Elisabeth
Mortensen (young woman train passenger), John Glover (Sammy), Lisa
Pelikan (young Julia), Susan Jones (young Lillian), Cathleen Nesbitt
(Julia's grandmother), Maurice Denham (undertaker), Mark Metcalf
(Pratt), Gérard Buhr (passport officer), Stefan Gryff (Hamlet), Lambert
Wilson (young man on train), Phillip Siegel (little boy in hospital),
Molly Urquhart (woman), Antony Carrick (butler), Ann Queensberry
(woman in Berlin station), Edmond Bernard (man in Berlin station),
Jacques David (fat man), Jacqueline Staup (woman in green hat), Hans
Verner (Vienna concierge), Christian De Tillière (Paris concierge), Jim
Kane (Sardi), Don Koll (first-nighter at Sardi's), Dick Marr (Sardi's
customer), and Shane Rimmer (customs officer)
Color
117 minutes

1982
FIVE DAYS ONE SUMMER
Ladd Company/Warner Brothers
Producer: **Zinnemann**
Executive Producer: Peter Beale
Director: **Zinnemann**
Screenplay: Michael Austin, from the short story, "Maiden, Maiden" by
Kay Boyle
Photography: Giuseppe Rotunno
Production Design: Willy Holt
Art Direction: Kathrin Brunner, Robert Cartwright, Don Dossett, Marc
Frédérix, Gérard Viard
Editing: Stuart Baird
Music: Elmer Bernstein

Cast: Sean Connery (Dr. Douglas Meredith), Betsy Brantley (Kate
Meredith), Lambert Wilson (Johann Biari), Jennifer Hilary (Sarah
Meredith), Isabel Dean (Kate's mother), Anna Massey (Jennifer Pierce),
Sheila Reid (Gillian Pierce), Gérard Buhr (Brendel), Georges Claisse
(Dieter), Kathy Marothy (Dieter's wife), Terry Kingley (Georg), Emilie
Lihou (old woman), Afred Schmidhauser (Martin), Jerry Brouwer (Van
Royen), Alexander John (Maclean), Michael Burrell (horse taxi driver),
Frank Duncan (first hut guardian), Robert Dietl (station master),
Günter Clemens (guide), Skil Kaiser-Passini (Eva), and Marc Duret,
François Caron, Benoît Ferreux (French students)
Color
108 minutes

FRED ZINNEMANN

INTERVIEWS

Revelations

I chose to do *Behold a Pale Horse*, because it's a very suspenseful and interesting story with very good, truthful characters; and the background is unusual. I liked the theme. The way the story is written the theme can come out very clearly.

The main theme is the story of a man who has the courage of his convictions. The title, *Behold a Pale Horse* is drawn from Revelations; it's very indicative of what the story is about. It's a story, an antagonism, with Manuel, a man who is an ex-guerrilla fighter, a refugee from Spain who lives in France twenty years after the civil war—he is played by Gregory Peck. The antagonist is Anthony Quinn who plays a Captain in the Spanish frontier police who is trying to catch him, and has been trying to catch him for twenty years. He lays a trap for him with his mother as bait. The third actor is Omar Sharif who plays a priest who has a story of his own, which is involved with the other two.

I liked the character of Manuel, the ex-guerilla leader, who in a sense is a modern Don Quixote—he is a very mystic character, very typically Spanish who believes that there are many things in the world that are more important than human lives including his own, and he thinks nothing of his own life in a sense. And this is quite true of all those people who sacrificed their lives as a gesture. He seemed to me very interesting. I also thought the Priest was very interesting but in quite a different way.

Originally published in *Films and Filming* 10.12 (September 1964): 5–6. Adapted from a tape-recorded interview.

The interplay of Manuel and the Police Captain—there is a great deal of tension in that relationship which was in a sense like Captain Ahab and Moby Dick. In addition to that, I thought the whole background was quite unusual and very promising. The combination of all these things made me want to do the picture.

Manuel is not a bandit. If you were to use modern termology you would say he's a kind of Robin Hood. When the Police Captain at the end says, "Why did he come back?" we did not want to give the answer ourselves, that is why we ended the picture with that question. And I find that almost everybody tends to answer it in his own way. There are some people who say he went back because he wanted to kill a man who informed on him, which is a valid enough reason. Some people say he went back, and in fact the character himself says, "What else can I do? " . . . and in a cafe scene he says, "Besides, they don't think that I can." It's a kind of defiance. You could say it's a man who temporarily has lost his courage as a result of his wounds who is trying to re-establish himself and regain his self-respect. There is the reason which some of my friends have advanced which is that the Priest really gets under the skin of Manuel who has been totally anti-church and who regarded anything to do with religion as utter nonsense. The Priest somehow persuades him that there is more to it, and it is conceivable that he returns over the border to try to protect the Priest, and stop him being arrested for having warned him of the trap being laid for him. So you can take your choice of any of these reasons according to your own likes.

I don't think his decision is a question of resignation. A comparison, which perhaps is a little far fetched, is last year in Saigon . . . nobody in the world knew really what was going on or why a man had to burn himself to death. Everybody said it must have been something very important for a person to decide to burn himself as a protest; it focused the attention of the world on it, and in some ways led to the downfall of the Diem regime of that time. This is only a general comparison— but in a sense Manuel's return to Spain and getting killed, you might say, is also a protest. When you say a protest against what, it is easy to answer, you can answer it yourself: it is a protest against oppression, against a police state . . . and this happens all the time, this is not fiction in that sense.

The scene when Manuel shoots the informer instead of the Police Captain has to do with what one thinks this particular character would do under those circumstances, and in my opinion Manuel, when faced with the choice of killing a life-long enemy or somebody who he considers is a traitor would kill the traitor. Perhaps in some way his enemy is an honourable adversary, but a traitor is like vermin.

The story itself is a composite story based on two or three stories that happened—the principal story that happened was about a terrorist who was killed in 1960. He was killed in circumstances vaguely resembling those that we portray in the film.

Religion is important to the extent that I've shown it; to the extent that a man who is a priest finds it possible to help someone who regards the priest as an arch enemy, who disregards his own personal safety and follows his own conscience. The Church and the political regime are at variants in the case shown in the film, as the priest will not go along with what the Police Officer represents. The Police Captain is not religious—he is superstitious: he is a man who when he starts to set up a trap for Manuel feels that he has to cover all bets; so he puts machine guns in the window, he puts detectives on the front steps of the hospital, he gets an observation post in a call-girl's apartment, and he goes into the church and buys two candles just in case God might do something for him. But I wouldn't call him religious because of this—the Priest is religious; the Captain is superstitious. When the Captain goes to Lourdes and says, "I'll give back the horse, and I won't see my mistress" it's, to my way of thinking, superstition not religion, of trying to make a deal.

We spent two months casting the film. We brought actors together from four countries: the United States, England, Italy and France. The interesting part was to blend it all together and see how it works and see if it could become a whole.

Casting varies entirely, it depends on what kind of picture you are doing, and there is no "method" to it. Sometimes you work on a story and you think about the character, but you can't find the right actor, then you happen to go to a play and you see a magnificent actor or actress and you suddenly feel that he is exactly who you want. Other times you see someone playing some sort of a part in a movie that is totally disconnected with the character that you have, but you feel that there is a facet that might be interesting and sometimes you take people like that. But there is no rule or regulation. Very often I've taken people who are totally unknown or sometimes people who are not even actors providing they were outgoing enough to be able to play themselves on the screen without being inhibited.

The way we cast Omar Sharif was very interesting. Before *Lawrence* came out David Lean told me about Omar Sharif. He said he was an absolutely marvellous actor, "If you possibly can take a look at him because he might be very good as the priest." So David was really the first person that talked about him. Sam Spiegel was the second. And I met Omar in New York when he was there for the opening of *Lawrence* and he seemed to be absolutely right just looking at him and that he would be very good. The priest in the story, as I wanted him, was very typically Spanish, with a quality of mysticism. Omar, to my knowledge, had not done anything of that kind before, but it was very evident that he had the quality I wanted, and he is a Catholic. And after we got together on the part he went to a Jesuit seminary and spent almost a week there just to get the frame of reference for the character. And when he came out he could really play a Spanish priest—priests from each country still reflect somehow the spiritual attitude of that country. An Italian or Irish priest, is quite different from a French or Spanish one, and it's fascinating to watch the fine points of difference. We wanted a Spaniard—and we got one! I think he is terrific. He's a young man, has an enormous capability, and should go very far, with the right parts.

Raymond Pellegrin is one of the finest actors I've ever worked with; I was delighted to have a man of that calibre for a part which was relatively small, that of the informer. He brought much more to it than the part deserved. If you had a mediocre actor playing a part like that, it becomes very one dimensional and it becomes just a plot device. But if you get a really fine artist like Pellegrin, he gives it a hint of much more depth, much more dimension to the character. He is able to fill in from his own imagination and certain things about it make you feel the character is really a human being instead of just a one dimensional heavy. My principle is always whenever I can get a really fine actor, to grab him because mediocrity is the thing to avoid.

The picture was shot in the studios in Paris and on location in the Pyrenees and near Biarritz. It was set up as a French production, and it seemed to be much more of one piece and easier to make that way. It was very important to bring local colour to the interiors as well as to the exteriors; and it was much easier to get the local colour in France than in Los Angeles.

I'd be perfectly happy to stay at home with moderate crews and things like that, but I find that I have to go where the story is. If the story has to be made in a certain place, that's where it has to be made. If you take *The Nun's Story,* for example, you *have* to go into the Belgian Congo to make it. I don't find any real disadvantages in being on location. Sometimes it's a very good thing, as in the case of *The Nun's Story.* It's very good away from the studio control. We were far into the jungle, and it was good because we were on our own.

Why did we change the title from that of the book, *Killing a Mouse on Sunday*? I've had an aversion to any title with the word "mouse" in it, which is probably because when I was very young the Mickey Mouse series of Disney started, and there's an association in my mind that anything to do with "mouse" has some kind of a feeling of a Disney cartoon, and that it is basically cute or coy or something like that. So I found this was totally against the meaning of the picture we were going to do. It's personal, in this case I didn't worry about what the audience would think, it's just that anything with the word "mouse" bothers me, and I found a lot of other people were bothered by it, and so we decided to change it, and came up with a title which we think expresses the feeling of the story much better. You can make a joke and say that the mouse was blown up into a horse!

In choice of subjects I don't aim for anything. It's almost as though, talking as a young man would, if you go out into the street you don't say now, "I'm going to start looking for a blonde who's six feet, three inches." I first have to read something that I get excited about, then I usually ask myself, "Why do I want to do it?" And that usually gives me a clue. Once I know why I want to do it, I know how to go about stress-ing the points that are exciting. It's the simplest way of analysis to say, "Why, what is it that makes me interested?"; and I go from there rather than the reverse way. I don't say, "Now I want to make a statement about the racial question."

I would love to do another western. I think I'd be very wary about doing another musical. But I'd love to do a western if I found a good story and if I could find good actors—they are getting very rare because it's becoming a sort of second-hand thing now with young actors, where the older ones, people like Gary Cooper, knew about the old west more from personal experience. The new ones have seen a lot of pictures and TV shows and it's a second-hand thing.

Zinnemann Talks Back

JAMES R. SILKE/1964

SILKE: *In writing about your films for* Cinema, *there has been some honest doubt in my mind as to what specifically Mr. Fred Zinnemann has been saying within his films over a period of time. There is common to each, I would say, an attempt at objectivism, which I don't believe is really practicable in cinema.*

ZINNEMANN: Well, I think we should start arguing right there. Because my own feeling is that it's a perfectly valid approach to present a problem or a question or an issue to an audience, and let them determine for themselves how they feel about it. I did that quite deliberately with *High Noon*. Quite deliberately. I felt it was very important to let the audience supply their own answers. I did the same thing, but quite deliberately, in *The Nun's Story*. Whether one liked the picture or not is perhaps not important. The important thing was that I felt it would be wrong to try to influence the audience for or against the institution of religious life. I did not want to propagandize one way or the other. That's why in the end, when the nun left the convent, I had no music, no comment of any sort. We had a large battle over that with the studio. The studio maintained that there should be music, that there's always music at the end of a picture. I finally said, well what should the music express? And that's when I had them, you see, because if it were triumphant music, it would say Warner Bros. is happy that the girl left the convent. If you had depressing music, it'd be lousy for an ending, obviously. So I made my point, and we left it up to the audience to decide whatever they wanted to decide.

Originally published in *Cinema* 2.3 (October–November 1964): 20–22, 30. Reprinted by permission of James R. Silke.

s: *Are you talking now about the comment on the religious institution or on the girl's attitude?*

z: Well, let me simplify: I didn't want a heavy or a hero in the story, because I didn't feel it was that kind of a story. I think it's always very simple to ask for rooting interest. There's no trick and anybody can do it. It's almost mechanical in the writing, in the way one directs the opening scenes. Rooting interest is something we all learned in kindergarten, because in the old days every picture was really based on it to the point where when you had a chase on horseback, the heavy was riding a black horse and the hero was riding a white horse, so you could tell who was which. But I'm not terribly concerned with heavies and heroes. I don't really believe in heavies and heroes personally. So perhaps that makes people think I'm not involved. I'm very involved in all kinds of things, but not on a black and white basis. I don't believe everybody stinks or that there are heroes and there are scoundrels. I think we're getting away from that point of view, at least I am.

s: *Well, that, of course, was my objection.*

z: You feel that one has to take sides, regardless.

s: *Not towards the social institution but toward the personality. I didn't know, for instance, in* High Noon, *whether Gary Cooper was inside a strong man or whether he sought his strength from exterior circumstances. This criticism, actually, is borrowed from a man named Howard Hawks. I don't know if he's expressed this to you or not. He said that he thought the Cooper character in* High Noon *was not a western character. And being an addict of the folklore of the West, I would agree with him. That kind of person really did not exist until much later in the West when there was that kind of dichotomy within the character. That is, sometimes he was moved by his society, sometimes he decided right from wrong because of the way he felt inside.*

z: I remember that in *Cinema*'s editorial you said why did Cooper run to a lot of people for help if in the end he was able to kill the heavies all by himself. Well, it seems to me that it's perfectly obvious that no one can tell ahead of time what the situation will be or how it will develop or whether he can cope with it all by himself. It seems the most natural thing in the world that in a situation like that a man would ask for help. Unless he had an ego that was so colossal that it surely would not be a western ego. So, frankly, I did not understand that whole position.

s: *My position was that Cooper would have gone out to find a professional killer to help him. Which is what usually happened in the West. Either that or he would have bought himself two shotguns and met the bad guys as they came off the train and killed them immediately.*
z: Well, I submit to you that at this point you're becoming a writer, you're no longer a critic.

s: *Well, of course, you're absolutely right.*
z: And here again, you're shifting your platform. When you're talking about how shall we tell this story, then we can discuss that. But we're talking about this particular thing as it stands and fortunately a lot of people did like it.

s: *I loved the film, I must admit.*
z: So there must be something to it that makes people identify with it. Now I maintain, and I will always maintain, that it's perfectly valid for a man who finds himself in a desperate situation to ask for help. And the fact that he's denied the help begins to work on his attitude. He becomes disillusioned or he grows up, or whatever else we want to say. But the fact that in his hour of need everybody is on the fence for one reason or another, and in the end he finds himself alone, that's really the crux of the story. The gun shooting that happened in the end is almost, you know, it's a deference to the traditional ending. But the whole story is the fact that a man asks for help and doesn't get it, for all kinds of reasons. That's what the picture is about in many ways. Now if you say this is not a western character, it's true. I wasn't there in 1860. Neither was Mr. Hawks. I'm sure he's a great scholar, I don't pretend to be a great scholar of western folklore, but I don't see what there is about the character that isn't valid. He's a man who's been marshal for a long time and is ready to quit and is getting married and wants to get out of town. At the last minute they tell him that this desperate emergency has come up. Conceivably a real westerner in the 1860s would have done something else, it's hard for me to say. I can't argue that point

with you. But I'd like you to elaborate on it a little, because I would love to understand it.

s: *Well, in taking Mr. Hawks' position in that case, the theme recurrent in Hawks' own films has to do with professional people. His characters are completely adequate, even if they're gangsters. Completely adequate. Thorough. They would not seek the help of the minister, the help of the congregation, or the help of a store clerk. There was one guy the* High Noon *marshal went after in the film which I thought was valid because the guy was also a fighter who knew the business of guns. Other than him anybody else would have been in the way as far as Cooper was concerned if he was a professional lawman. This happened when Earp went after the Clantons. And when they hired a marshal in Dodge they got the best gunfighter. They didn't take anybody—the minister, the teacher or a clerk—they found a man who was a professional with guns to handle that job for them. And he in turn would hire cutthroats. Or, if he couldn't handle it that way, he would not worry about it, he would find himself a double-barreled shotgun and shoot the outlaws as soon as he saw them. And there was no chivalry involved, if that was his extremity. Now I think that, as a storyteller about the West, that would have been more honest, I guess, to Mr. Hawks and to me about the West. But* High Noon *was compelling. This is the point that I tried to raise in the articles, too, the film was compelling despite its divergences. The* Sundowners *too was one of the most beautiful films I've seen in a long time. And I don't know just why. I can't say to myself what was compelling about these characters. Perhaps it's that they are so real. You make a great attempt I would say at reality. Is that my own interpretation or—*

z: The only way I can put it is that if a character in a situation does something, I want to know why. I'm not interested in a man shooting a gun, I'm interested in why he does it. And perhaps this is the difference between *High Noon* and some other westerns, I don't know. The action as such fascinates me, but by itself it's nothing to me. The only thing I care about is why does a person do something, what is it that makes him do it. This to me is the whole drama. And then the person, and the conflict of the person, become the landscape that I work from, you know? Now, in those terms I think we can't really talk about realism, because I believe human beings are human beings and to the best of my ability I try to understand them and show the way I see them.

In the case of *The Sundowners*, I was very moved by the book. The book had the feelings of a love story between two people who had been married for a long time. I thought it was marvelous to see, for once, people who've been married for fifteen or eighteen years and stayed in love with each other under very rough circumstances. I thought this was enough basis for a movie, right or wrong, and so I took the chance and did it. In *The Nun's Story*, I was fascinated by the idea that one person who had taken final vows and promised to be a nun for life discovered that she was not cut out to be a nun, and then had the courage to go through the steps that were necessary to get out. Then I met the real person of the book, and this determined me even more to do the picture because when you talk about heroism, there's a kind of moral heroism there that's utterly tremendous, admirable. This might sound very highfalutin'. I don't know, but this is the way I feel.

s: *Could you give me the character, for instance, in* Pale Horse. *The one played by Peck?*

z: Yes. The character in *Pale Horse* on one level is a man like a modern Don Quixote, a guy who tilts against windmills. It's very Spanish, and I think very human. On another level he's an aging man whose whole life is surrounded by a big question mark as to his own personal courage. He is a man who is looking for his own balls. You might say, he has just about lost 'em and he gets them back in the end by what he does. And what he does is again a very Spanish gesture which hopefully the audience here will understand. I don't know whether they will or won't. The crux of the story is in a scene in a café where a friend of his says, your mother is already dead, it's too late now to see her and yet you still want to go back into the policeman's trap. Why are you going back? And he says, what else can I do? And then he says, besides, I want to show them, because they don't think that I can. Now, to me, this is very moving, very moving and very valid. And I'm very concerned with problems of people who struggle for their self-respect or their dignity as human beings or their convictions. You know, all of that to me is very important. Now, granted it sounds academic when one talks about it and granted it sounds remote, and probably is, you know.

s: *Could it be said that within each of these films there is a concern upon the part of the central character for his own self-respect?*

z: Yes, self-respect and conviction. If you trace all of my stories . . .
you can take *High Noon*, you can take *From Here to Eternity*. In the case
of *From Here to Eternity*, it's the individual against the large organization
. . . and there's the man who says, I don't want to box, because I killed
somebody or blinded somebody and I'm through with it, no matter
what, you can't make me. And they try to bribe him, and he won't box.
And he says, a man has got to do what he's got to do. Which is the
same thing in a sense and in the end he gets killed more or less as a
direct outgrowth of that. In *High Noon* again, a man who is leaving
town, and at a certain point stops and says, I've got to go back. And the
wife says, why are you going back? And he says, I don't know. And he
goes back. Basically, it's something that concerns me very much.

s: *There is a conquest then within each character really. He does find self-*
respect almost in each case.
z: Yes. But the important thing is that he doesn't really know he's
looking for it. Because if he did, then I think you'd have a lousy movie.
It'd be a flat, preachy, crummy kind of a picture and the whole thing is
that he must not know about it.

s: *Then, in effect, you are telling the story Hawks would pick up after the*
end of your movie. In other words, his characters start with this position.
They know what they're about, who they are, and what they have done, and
what they can accomplish. There's no question in their mind. A perfect John
Wayne type of character.
z: Wonderful! Wonderful! I admire Hawks very much. I only wish
he'd leave my films alone! But actually, you see, I think that each man
has his own sphere of interest and his own way of looking at the world,
and I respect and admire his enormously. But it'd be idiotic for me to
try to imitate it, even if I wanted to, you know, which I don't.

s: *Without these obvious black and white characterizations, your exposi-*
tion to the audience is the struggle within the character to find himself or his
own self-respect.
z: Yes. And I like the conflict inside the character which I think is terribly important. In other words, I'm not really interested in somebody
who knows what he's about. Because it bores me. I like to see a man

who goes through some kind of crisis, and as a result, something opens up for him, he begins to understand something that perhaps he didn't understand before. I don't believe that human beings can go through life untouched and knowing all about themselves. And the older I get, the more certain I am. It's not human.

S: *Now, do all the characters within your films behave pretty much in that manner?*

Z: The protagonist has to behave in that manner. As for the antagonist, if I can avoid his being a villain, I like it very much. In *Pale Horse*, the antagonist is the captain of the Guardia Civil, which is the frontier police. He is really a man who is just doing his job. And to many of us he's a heavy. But he's perfectly justifiable from the other point of view. And we tried not to show him as a heavy, even though in the end he traps and kills the protagonist. I don't see what one gains by having these heavies, you know. To my mind today they become a little ridiculous. There are terribly few people in the world that I would look at and say, this person is a monster and there's nothing human about him.

S: *But then there are those people! Even though we live in a very ill-defined time when such things are becoming debatable.*

Z: Yes, there are people who appear against each other and kill each other without knowing why. In any war, there's no reason except that they have one kind of uniform and the others have some other kind of uniform and they kill each other. When you ask why, it goes back to the old thing in *All Quiet on the Western Front* when the soldiers sit there, and they try to figure out why, and somebody says, do you mean to say that a mountain in Germany gets mad at a river in France? And there are a lot of questions like that that I think are going to become increasingly important now. I think the era has passed when we can easily and flatly say this guy is a bastard and this guy is great, you know? It just isn't like that at all. And this is why, going back to the mechanics of picture making, I repeat, it's a very easy thing to develop rooting interest. We tell the audience you've got to be for this guy, and you've got to be against this man. If you do it skillfully enough, they'll be happy to do it for you. But, right or wrong, I don't like to do it. It takes something away from my way of looking at pictures and looking at the world. And I must confess that I think pictures are probably a good deal more successful and make a lot more money if the rooting interest is more black and white, so that the audience can say hurray the good man is winning! The other way there is more of a state of confusion, but I believe it mirrors more closely the state of the world today, because I'm never quite sure what's what.

s: *Then you are in a sense acting as yourself.*
z: I'm saying to the audience look at this, what do you think, how do you feel about it? Curiously enough some audiences like it very much. *Pale Horse* ends with a question when Quinn says to his assistant, you made a trap for him, why did he come back? And the question is never answered. They just look at each other, and they don't know.

s: *Yet you're not consciously trying to reflect the times, you're concerned still essentially with the character?*
z: Yes.

s: *The individual pictured living in this kind of a situation. Well, I'd say you have fairly well analyzed your own approach to picture making which most directors refuse to do.*
z: I don't like usually to talk an awful lot, you know, but I thought it was useful to clarify it because *Cinema's* article did worry me a bit. It gave me pause when I read I was the maker of anti-films, or anti-movies.

s: *This, of course, was not* Cinema's *own comment. This is a comment that has been made, however.*
z: I know.

s: *You were producer and director on* Pale Horse. *Were circumstances such that you were able to make this film as you wished to make it?*
z: Yes.

s: *You will have the final cut?*
z: Absolutely.

S: *Has this always been the case?*

Z: No. No, as you know, it's a function of growing up. If I can be cynical for a minute, it has to do with making at least two pictures that are very successful at the box office and also get very good reviews and are respected. If you can have two, then you're okay and you can do more or less what you want, until you make two in succession that have lousy reviews and are flops. And then you are more or less back where you started.

S: *I was concerned with whether you had this autonomy. I'm glad to know that you do, because there's a lot of bellyaching about the fact that no director has it in Hollywood, for instance.*

Z: Have you read *Cahiers du Cinema*? You obviously read these things. You may have read the French film makers' roundtable discussion in which it was said that since directors have become independent of the major studios in the last ten years and have much more liberty, their pictures are a lot worse than they were before. And the panelists proceed to elaborate, you know, and take one director after another.

S: *Talking about American directors?*

Z: American, yes. It's just about American movies, and they say all these guys who in the '30s and '40s when the studios forced them to take a certain cast and a picture couldn't be more than an hour and a half and what not, all these men made magnificent pictures. Now that the discipline has been relaxed, their pictures are not as good. And the panelists go down the line, and in a very cynical and sophisticated way they proceed to prove their point. It's rather, interesting, you'll have to take a look.

S: *Was Truffaut in on that?*

Z: I forget. Godard I remember was part of it. Man by the name of Pierre Kast. What amused me especially is that most of these guys have made pictures that are absolutely ghastly. Rivette made a film that shouldn't happen to a dog. Pierre Kast made a movie that, if I had made this picture, I would crawl under a rock and hide. You know, it's so pretentious and so lousy and then he tries to save it by playing Beethoven underneath and some really good music, you know. And then another gentleman made a very, very questionable picture and finally had to make a sex scene to get people to look at it. I admire that kind of gall, you know, for them to be the spokesmen for the cinema. I think it gives you all kinds of distortions.

s: *They do favor the American directors, though, very highly in France.*
z: Yes, Hawks and Hitchcock are very, very big. One wonders why Huston isn't. I mean, it's a peculiar way to judge people when you don't take the totality of his work. They take a man like John Huston who's made *Sierra Madre, Maltese Falcon*, tremendous pictures during the war, and they sort of dismiss him in a very patronizing way just because the last two or three pictures weren't very good. I don't understand that kind of criticism, I think it's odd, you know.

s: *I'd maintain that a strong director any time within the history of the cinema one way or another has been able to get his films the way he wanted them. Whether it's John Ford, who shoots just enough film so you've got to cut it one way and that's it. Whether he, like Hitchcock, plans it out so carefully that you know what you're going to get. Art work has got to have a strong personality behind it. And then, even if there are many controls, whether it be the Pope, MGM or Louis B. Mayer, the artist has the tenacity to get it done.*
z: Absolutely right. Next to talent, stubbornness is the most important thing a director can have, has to have, *has* to have . . . to know what he wants and to stick with it, no matter what.

s: *In making films today is there any control over a director in this sense: Does the film have to cost a certain amount of money? Can you make a film for three million dollars and also make one for three hundred thousand dollars? Will they back the one as easily as the other?*
z: Yes.

s: *For you, for Fred Zinnemann.*
z: Yes. They would back it regretfully. They would say, why do you want to make a little picture? But if I insist, they would do it.

s: *The pattern would be towards the big picture?*
z: Always. Because, as businessmen, they would think in terms of time and the fact that in the time that I make a little picture, I could

make a big one and they could get more money. That is perfectly legitimate from their point of view, though it seems kind of silly when you talk about it. But that's what business is about. From their point of view it is to their advantage if I make big pictures that promise big profits rather than a small picture that may satisfy my ego but would bring nothing to the company financially.

s: *How did* The Search *do as a small film?*
z: It did very well because it was made for $250,000, and it made quite a lot of money. Now do you feel that *The Search* was uncommitted? Because obviously here I took great pains to just present the thing without any comment whatsoever.

s: *No, I felt it was committed. When you get down to my exact thinking, I felt that* High Noon *was committed because of the personality of Gary Cooper. You know that the potential was there. And I felt like that all the way through* The Search *and I can't recall exactly why. Maybe it was because of the great sympathy that Montgomery Clift had at that time as a performer. I don't know what it was exactly.*
z: Some of these things happen subconsciously. I don't know either except I know that I spent almost three months going to D.P. camps and talking to people who had just come out of the concentration camps and talking to kids and unwell people and the sum total of what I heard was so overwhelming that you couldn't help but reproduce some of it. You could not *not* get it on the film, you know.

s: *Your sense of newsreel documentary in that film, as I recall it now, was great. Of course, you had the wartime rubble and all those things which gave a great sense of believability. And I understand that for* Pale Horse *you hired the cameraman who shot the Hungarian revolution.*
z: Yes, Jean Badal. He made two films before he worked with me.

s: *Do you particularly like this documentary approach? How does it aid your theme?*
z: It depends always entirely on the subject matter and on what style you are after. And *Pale Horse*, I felt again, should be reminiscent of a newsreel, because I felt it would be more immediate that way. In a sense, I was trying to show the story without intruding as the camera

does when you photograph an event in a newsreel. In *High Noon*, it was the same thing, because I remember Floyd Crosby, and I decided to photograph it as though it were a newsreel of the period. We studied the Mathew Brady photographs of the Civil War enormously to see this white sky, you know. Up to that time it was more or less mandatory to have a pretty grey sky with pretty white clouds in it, and we deliberately used flat lighting for Cooper to make him look as moth-eaten as we could which was then a great departure for a western hero. And we got a lot of complaints while we were shooting. The front office said, this is ghastly photography, get another cameraman.

s: *Would you say of this particular style which I associate with you as a visual kind of look, would you say you did not necessarily imitate it in* The Sundowners?
z: Huh uh.

s: *There was a great sense of land, however, in* The Sundowners.
z: Yes, well, that was more of a romantic story to me, and I tried to play it as romantic as I could. I had a man who's a great cameraman in a romantic sense. He'd done *Summertime* with David Lean–Jack Hilliard, he's a wonderful cameraman. Very romantic. And so all of that was done in that style, you might say.

s: *Did you let Hilliard then impose his creative style in that area? Is this a conceivable thing for a director to do?*
z: Oh yes, absolutely. For me, yes, I like to get the maximum contribution from everybody who works with me. That's why I try to get the most talented people in every department whether actors, writers, cameramen, musicians, whatever. I depend on what they bring to it, and I supply the direction. But I want a maximum contribution. Otherwise I could do it all by myself.

s: *You would say then that the visual look of the film could change in a Zinnemann film from picture to picture?*
z: Yes, it could, absolutely. I don't know if you saw *The Nun's Story* but there the photography also was romantic actually in color. It certainly didn't have a newsreel feeling about it. It was all colors.

S: *There are certain directors—Von Sternberg comes to mind immediately or Hitchcock—with whom the manner in which they shoot film is always consistent. There's a graphic look that belongs to the director solely.*

Z: To me it's no use. You see, I don't feel the need for a trademark in that sense. I would not get an enormous kick out of it if somebody after looking at a picture for two minutes could say, this is a Zinnemann picture. It would probably please me, but basically I don't think it matters one way or the other. I think it's a conceit, you know.

S: *My commitment, personally, as a critic, would not be either way. Of course, some directors feel they can tell more visually and have more the individuality of the painter. For instance, Fellini, Kurosawa. Others are more concerned with a story. Even Hitchcock's look is kind of innocuous. It's more his cutting, I guess.*

Z: But Hitchcock has a marvelous style when you think of *Rebecca*, for instance.

S: *Well, it's there, but it's difficult to pinpoint. It's not flamboyant.*

Z: No, that's right, it's not pronounced, you don't feel it. Perhaps, you know, I haven't examined myself, but I think perhaps the reason that I don't push it is because that isn't the most important thing that I want to bring forward in a picture. When I do a movie, there are other things that perhaps are more important to me, and I would rather be as unobtrusive as possible, except where there's a specific reason to be otherwise.

S: *There's a tendency in criticism to become dogmatic about any one of these phases, yet there are so many areas of control open to the director that the fact is that his own personality is going to find expression in one way or another. That I feel has to happen.*

Z: Of course.

S: *But that it doesn't have to find expression in each direction completely, of course, is obvious.*

Z: No. Above everything else, I don't believe in ever making a movie to prove anything to anybody or to prove anything to myself. The only reason I like to make a movie is because it moves me, the material one way or another excites me, and then I hope to be able to transmit that emotion to the audience. But to me, everything else is a mannerism, you know, and I admire it if it's brilliantly done but I think it's a kind of slickness, and it's not of the essence. And what I really want to do more and more is to strip things down to the essentials. This is why I prefer working in black and white rather than color. And I'd rather work on a small screen than a big screen, because I think all these things are not of the essence, you know.

s: *How important to Fred Zinnemann at this point is it to have a big star? Could you make a film without any stars? Would the bankers, the studio permit it?*
z: It depends on the story, it depends entirely on what you are after, but of course, you can. You see, from the studio's point of view, if I make a film with someone like Gregory Peck, that would cost one kind of budget. If I make a film with someone that's unknown, it would be another budget. But I'm convinced that they would let me try to do it, unless it was in their eyes so wildly far out that they couldn't in good conscience risk even a small amount. But I think there is a tendency to go by the judgment of people who in some way or another have at least proven that they have some sense about what they are doing. If I came to Columbia, let's say, and said here is a story that you may not like very much but it can be done for two hundred thousand dollars with unknowns, I think they would go along. With some reluctance, but I believe they would go.

s: *This is the point where I feel there has been a change. Until recently the thinking seemed to be, first we'll get a big star, then we'll think about who to sign as director. Now I would say there's more of a tendency to consider the director first and his career, the success of it. Do you see any change in this?*
z: It's been an enormous improvement. More and more of the studios here have become conscious of the director's contribution. Two companies, Columbia and United Artists, really back directors to a tremendous extent. Columbia backed me to an unbelievable extent in *Pale Horse* when we developed trouble with the Spanish government. They really were terribly good about it.

s: *I've noticed that with those two companies, too, they seem to be explor-*
ing with young directors and with better established directors, and taking
more chances.

z: They are very forward looking and they have a courage and enthusiasm I don't think the other companies share to that degree. It's much
easier in these two companies to start as a young director.

s: *Have you made attempts to get any control over your advertising?*

z: I have more than a courtesy voice in it, but I'm not very good at it.
It's not my racket. I know what makes an ad that I like or dislike, but
that may not at all be the ad that will bring people to the box office. So
my tendency is to stay away from it as much as I can.

s: *Do they listen to you?*

z: Oh, they do. They ask me all kinds of questions. They seem to take
certain things that I say, but I've made it very plain from the beginning
that I didn't know much about it. I don't believe in passing myself off
as an expert and then making some fatal mistake, because I really don't
understand it.

s: *I feel bad advertising can be a tremendous detriment to the business.*

z: That's what killed us with *Sundowners* you know, because they sold
it as a sex picture. And all the sex addicts went and were disappointed.

s: *Do you use a production designer and design a film or pre-cut it in that*
sense?

z: I have used them, but I find that nowadays, especially, I would just
as soon do my own thumbnails and use them as the key from which I
move. Because these things are so personal and so important to me that
if the designer does them they may look marvelous, but they're never
quite what I want. Almost never.

s: *You then make your own drawings. Do you then proceed to shoot what is*
known as the establishing shot, a middle shot, the group, and you pre-select a
host and so it's almost pre-cut?

z: Oh, sure. In other words, if there's a person on a train arriving at a
station and we do the scene from his or her point of view, I'm not

going to make a long shot in which you see the station and the train
pulling in, you know. I put the camera in the train and photograph the
person in the foreground as we see the approaching station. In that
sense, no, I never believe in establishing shots. It's a curious thing in
Pale Horse. In the beginning we had to do a brief prologue showing the
Spanish Civil War, when it started and when it ended, because it had
bearing on Peck's character. And we found some wonderful newsreel
material which we used. And then the job became finding a way to do a
scene of Peck who at the end of the war is about to cross the border
into France to become a refugee, an exile. We shot this scene in the
mountains, but then it became a question of making it fit the rest of
the film. And we duped it several times over until it became as spare of
detail as newsreel shots do. And now you can't tell the difference and
when you see Peck, you don't believe it quite for the first few feet, you
know. That worked out well, I thought. It's very tricky though. They
have to watch every print they make at the lab, because it's a very tricky
effect to get.

s: *So you really in your mind then, and with your sketches, know exactly
what you're going to shoot and what you're going to need. Or do you shoot
excess in certain scenes?*
z: Not always. I like to have a very firm skeleton of the overall and of
each scene. But within that I like to leave it to chance, because I find so
many things happen that you can take advantage of. I hate not to use
certain things that present themselves. I'd rather be alert enough to
make a change and adjust and incorporate. So instead of shooting a lot
of takes on each scene I like very much to get the first and second takes
and get a performance that perhaps isn't polished but has spontaneity.
That to me is very important. The more spontaneous it is, I feel, the
closer it comes to truthfulness, before the actor has time to think about
it and polish it, which is different of course from the theater. The stage
is entirely, something entirely different.

s: *Are you going to go ahead with* Hawaii *at this point?*
z: No, no. I'm out of that. George Roy Hill is going to direct it.

S: *What is your next project?*

Z: I don't know. Possibly I'll do a TV picture for the United Nations which would be designed to show how the United Nations contributes to maintaining the peace. If it's done, it would be a story about a group of United Nations soldiers, either Irish or Canadians or South Africans or something like that, or Swedes. Possibly in the Congo . . . and it would be not a documentary but a fiction based on true incidents. It should convey, without pushing it, the idea that the United Nations can local-ize small wars that could otherwise explode into an overriding total war. This is one of the most important functions they have, which a lot of people don't seem to accept, you know. If that comes up, I'd do that towards the end of the year.

S: *Did you ever do anything like that before?*

Z: Yes, for various reasons. I made a documentary picture once. It was a fund-raising picture for the Children's Hospital here. It was called *Benjy*. It had to do with a kid who was sick. And it brought me one of the greatest compliments paid me on a picture. When we ran the first cut, the projectionist came out and said, where do I send my money?

Some Questions Answered

A C T I O N / 1 9 6 7

ACTION: *Do you have any preference in the type of movies you like to direct?*
FRED ZINNEMANN: No, I don't. I like to do what excites me. If I read something or see something that I find moving and exciting it starts right there. I have no prearranged ideas as to what I would like to do.

ACTION: *After becoming a hyphenate, as they call the double-doers, does the producer side of you ever battle with the director side?*
FZ: I try to avoid that. It would paralyze me. What I try to do is have as good an executive producer as I can get. It usually works out very well. He is the financial-administrative conscience. I let him worry about contracts and all business details. The great function of a man like that, of course, is to give me elbow room and let me worry about making the picture. I couldn't go through the actual functions of making deals and all that without going mad. I don't think anybody can do both jobs at the same time.

ACTION: *I notice that in almost all of your films, only one screenwriter is listed. Is that a matter of preference or just good luck?*
FZ: It's good luck, I suppose. But it is also a matter of casting, just like with actors. You try very hard to get the right person and then you stay with him, stay with him and keep trying until it works. I'm not too much in favor of the committee system—it gets to be too impersonal.

Originally published in *Action* (June 1967): 22–23. Reprinted by permission of the Directors Guild of America, Inc.

ACTION: *Did you and the writer ever feel that the ending of* The Nun's Story *might have been more reverential if the girl had come back to the church?*

FZ: No. I think it would be sentimental. I think the truth was that the young lady realized that she could no longer obey, and she drew the only possible consequence. I think if we tried for a happy ending it would have been deplorable.

ACTION: *If you could determine the length of* From Here to Eternity *yourself, how long would it run?*

FZ: Not run more than two hours and fifteen minutes. Even though at the time we were making it, we were complaining about Harry Cohn's insistence on a two hour film, I think he had a very good idea. I remember in the old days the saying was that pictures should be made short enough so that the audiences would leave saying they wished it had been a little longer. I think we send them in the opposite direction quite often now.

ACTION: *If you were to re-edit* The Nun's Story, *especially the first half which documents the training of the novices and postulants, would you trim it? Do you think it is overlong?*

FZ: I feel that I would keep it exactly as it is. Curiously enough I originally thought it was a bit slow. But seeing it again tonight, I feel that it is correct. I think it is the right pace for what it depicts. And I think it really portrays and reflects correctly what it set out to do—to tell the story of a spiritual struggle, one which should not be defined in terms of action. I was watching the audience. It seemed to me that up to the Congo scene almost everyone sat fairly still, but then people started scratching and moving around. I would make some cuts there—the African part is too long and should have been trimmed. And the leprosy sequence should have come out.

ACTION: *In several of your films, I believe, you have used non-actors. How difficult is it working with people who have no acting experience?*

FZ: Well, it depends. If you work with non-professionals, the most important thing is that they should, as people, not be inhibited. If they are outgoing people and not too self-conscious, and if you are not asking them to play characters other than themselves and if you let them stay within their own respective frames of reference, you will find that there is not too much trouble—provided that you don't ask them to do it too often. If they do a piece of action once or twice, it is fine. After that they can sort of hear themselves talk, and it becomes very stiff and lifeless.

ACTION: *Have you been influenced by the work or advice of other directors?*
FZ: I've learned an enormous amount from a number of Hollywood directors by watching their work religiously and one of the great ones to me was John Ford. I've always looked up to him as a great picture maker. Ford saw a couple of my early pictures and one day he said to me, "You know, you could be a pretty good director if you'd stop fooling around with that boom and quit moving the camera so much." And then he said, "To me, the camera is an information booth. I like to keep it still and have the characters come to it and tell their story. I don't move the camera unless there is a very, very good reason for it." I think this accounts for the wonderful simplicity of story-telling that Ford has—and the wonderful discipline and organization of his pictures. I feel that one of the terrible things in Hollywood is that the great directors who made this industry what it is are forgotten as soon as they stop functioning. The lack of feeling for tradition is a terrible thing.

ACTION: *Mr. Zinnemann, what happens to a picture when it's on television and is broken up with commercials?*
FZ: What happens to it shouldn't happen to a dog. I do hope we find a way of doing something about this butchering they do with pictures. I think it is an outrage.

ACTION: *Have you changed your directing style over the past ten years or so to adjust to the changes in subject matter?*
FZ: I'm not conscious of changing my style. I try to look at each new story as a new challenge, so to speak. And the style develops from the approach to the picture, the material itself. I have never consciously tried to change my style.

ACTION: *In regard to wide screens, for instance?*

FZ: I've worked as little with widescreen as I can. I am very old fashioned. If I had my way I would work in black and white on 16 mm film.

ACTION: *Do you find actors who use the "method" more difficult to work with than say, a man like Paul Scofield, who is part of the English classical school?*

FZ: There is a great difference in the way they work. I have found that actors who had trained the way Scofield did to be more flexible and more readily adaptable, and that their technique has a wider range than the young American actors brought up in the method. On the other hand, the young American actors are capable of an enormous intensity in the way they work because they personalize everything. Most of the English actors feel that this is wrong; they don't look at the character in their own terms. They don't say, "What would I do if I were in that situation?" They try to put themselves into the character before they start acting and reacting. Of course, they have a lot more stage training, which is enormously important. They have a very sharp sense of timing which comes from being in front of a live audience all the time.

ACTION: *Filming properties which were originally stage plays, notably* A Man for All Seasons, *what special techniques do you employ to make them cinematic?*

FZ: The most important thing is to try to cut all the dialogue that is not essential, and to try *not* to play as much *on* the dialogue as *off* the dialogue. In other words play *between* the lines—on the reactions and thoughts of the people rather than on the spoken word. You may have noticed that there are a great many close-ups—the main thing is not to have the dialogue merely rattled off, but rather to show what the characters feel and what they think.

If the actors in the film are those who were in the play, you have to work with them in such a way as to prevent them from projecting. Normally, in stage plays, you know, actors have to project across the footlights in order to be able to reach the audience in the balcony. The difference in film is, of course, that the actors speak to each other rather than to the audience.

ACTION: *Would you compare working with Marlon Brando with Montgomery Clift?*

FZ: They had one thing in common—they were both enormously talented men, probably the two most talented actors I have ever worked with. I would say that Monty was an actor of greater discipline than Brando. Marlon tends very often to play to himself whereas Monty always played to the other people. It was also easier to shape Monty's performance because he tended to go along with one's ideas whereas Marlon, of course, has very strong ideas of his own. And it is sometimes not easy to penetrate that. Even though at the time we made *The Men*, his first film, he was quite amenable. But by comparison Clift was an easier actor to work with.

ACTION: *How did you happen to pick Frank Sinatra for the part of Maggio in* From Here to Eternity?

FZ: I didn't. He picked himself. The minute word got out that we were going to make the picture, Sinatra started bombarding everybody with telegrams—Harry Cohn, the president of Columbia Pictures at the time, Buddy Adler, the producer, Dan Taradash, the writer, and myself. Once a week each of us would get a cable signed "Maggio." He didn't sign "Sinatra." He was convinced that he was the man for the part, and he was determined to play it. We actually favored another actor, a very fine one—Eli Wallach. Eli made a very good test, a marvelous test, but it turned out that he had a previous commitment with Kazan, to do *Camino Real* on Broadway. So he dropped out, and we made a test with Sinatra, and it turned out very well. Harry Cohn, by the way, a marvelous businessman, had Sinatra come all the way from Nairobi, from Kenya—at his own expense—to do the test. And then he paid him $8000 for the whole part.

The Lone Wolf and the Jackal

PAUL R. MICHAUD/1972

"*The Day of the Jackal*," said director Fred Zinnemann about his latest film, "was made purely as entertainment and doesn't pretend to be anything else. It should not be taken seriously politically or in any other way, because it's just a technical exercise in suspense." The film, based on Frederick Forsyth's best-selling novel about a plot to assassinate Charles de Gaulle, was Zinnemann's first picture since 1966 when he won the Academy Award for *A Man for All Seasons*, and he was obviously pleased with the way it turned out. "I had a marvelous time making it," he said smiling. "I would say that it came out 95 percent as I had hoped it would—which is more than one has the right to hope for, actually.

"I liked the challenge of having a piece of suspense in which you know the ending. You know that de Gaulle is not killed. That's what excited me about the book, and I think most people who read it had the same reaction. I was especially fascinated by the technique the author used. He never told you how or what was going to happen, and following that style we always tried not to let the audience get ahead of us."

Directing *The Day of the Jackal* came about almost by chance. After his success with *A Man for All Seasons* he began work on *Man's Fate* based on André Malraux's novel about the Chinese Civil War. "I had an enormous, enormous need to do *Man's Fate*," he said sadly, "because that book was a bible to us in my generation. It was one of the great novels of the '30s and '40s, and to be asked to make a film of it was one of the greatest events of my life." Unfortunately, after three years and $5 million, MGM cancelled the project as an economy measure.

Published by permission of Paul R. Michaud.

Zinnemann spent the next two years looking for other projects until one day when he stopped in at producer John Woolf's office. "I saw this manuscript sitting on his desk—it was very fat—so I asked him if I could read it, and he said yes. I didn't know what it was about—the book hadn't been published yet—but I took it home and read it over night. The next day I asked Woolf if I could do it, and he said yes."

Finding someone to play the hired killer, the Jackal, was not very difficult. "I wanted the Jackal to be very unobtrusive," Zinnemann explained. "I wanted him to be a man who could get lost in a crowd, so I didn't want a big name star for the part. After all, if I used a famous star, the audience would wonder why the police didn't ask him for his autograph." He finally decided on Edward Fox for the role.

"I had a very clear idea of what I was after. I felt the Jackal should come across as being an upper-class Englishman who was probably the second son of some very important noble family, who probably went into the army, probably later on became a mercenary in the Congo or Algeria, and then continued his life as a hired killer when the mercenary business fell off. Physically, the prototype was the master spy Kim Philby. I saw a photograph of him once. He was a very handsome, rather cold-looking young man with great style. I felt that that was the kind of man I wanted to find. Then I saw Edward Fox in the film *The Go Between* where he played an aristocrat and played him very well. He had one line, I remember, that impressed me very much. He said 'Nothing is ever a lady's fault,' and he said it with such conviction that I knew he had to be a very good actor. Fox was very, very easy to direct. Usually actors who are at the beginning of their careers are very cooperative." This is something that Zinnemann should know. Two young actors who had their screen debuts in Zinnemann films were Montgomery Clift in *The Search* (1948) and Marlon Brando in *The Men* (1950).

As was the case with most of his films, *The Day of the Jackal* was shot almost entirely on location in order to make the film as realistic as possible. "It's very important to reinforce a story that is supposed to be true with as much essential truthfulness as possible," he said. Therefore, the climactic search for the Jackal during the Bastille Day celebration was actually filmed at the Fourteenth of July parade in Paris. "We had police permission and special passes so we could go through the lines with our hand-held cameras and the actors. When we filmed the detective searching for the killer, there was the parade and the tanks and the people in the background. Something like that could never be staged. The problems came later, when we wanted to film de Gaulle in front of the Arch of Triumph. 'De Gaulle' by the way was an actor who specializes in impersonating de Gaulle. He knows every little detail about the man: how he walks, how he stands, what he does. But in order to shoot this properly, we wanted to rent the same enormous flag that hung down from the Arch during the parade. We wanted to shoot this scene in August, but it turned out that the people who rented the flag were on a holiday, so we waited for them to return at the end of the month."

Though such attention to detail might seem somewhat extravagant, the wait for the right flag was only one of many examples of Zinnemann's obsession with authenticity. Earlier in the film there was a brief shot—no more than five seconds—of some of the characters standing in front of the old train station, the Gare Montparnasse. The only problem with this was that the old station had been torn down and a modern skyscraper built in its place. Naturally, Zinnemann rebuilt part of the old station. "What we did was to rebuild the lower floor of the Gare Montparnasse, the entrance to the metro station, and the little house for people who were waiting for the bus. And the Parisians, who loved the old station and hated the new tower got all excited. 'They're going to tear down the tower,' they said, and they would go into the little house and wait for the buses that never came."

If attention to detail is essential to his work, the heart of the detail comes from extensive research. "I love to do background research," he said. "The more, the merrier. You start going, and you can't stop. It's like an archeological expedition. You bore a shaft into something, and it branches out in all directions. You find connections that are unheard of. And that in itself is totally fascinating. It's one of the most exciting parts of motion picture making. I remember making *The Nun's Story*. Since I am not a Catholic, everything I had to learn was new to me. At first I didn't know where to begin, but once we got into the ramifications of what a religious community was all about and how it operates and hangs together, we got more and more involved. We spent two years just researching *The Nun's Story*, and it was more fun than actually making the movie."

Zinnemann's passion for authenticity comes from his early training, and it is a trait that has remained with him all his life. The first film he worked on while still a young man in Germany was *Menschen am Sonntag* (1929), a semi-documentary he made with Billy Wilder and Robert Siodmak. The film owed much of its style to Robert Flaherty—cinema's most important documentary film maker—who later was to become Zinnemann's mentor. "Just listening to Flaherty talk was a liberal education for me," the sixty-six-year-old director recalled many years later, speaking of the time they worked together. "After I went out on my own, I really wanted to work very much the way Flaherty did with films like *Moana* and *Nanook of the North*. It just didn't work out that way though, and gradually I went into feature films and became a Hollywood director." However, even as a director of commercial films, he maintained his ties with the documentary form. In 1938 and 1951 he won Academy Awards for his documentary shorts, and many of his successful fiction films were semi-documentaries. In *The Men*, for example, a film about paraplegic war veterans, he did much of the filming in a Los Angeles V.A. hospital, using real patients in many of the roles. "I wanted people who would be behaving, rather than acting," he said.

Sometimes, of course, his desire for realism worked against his subject as with his film of *Oklahoma!* (1955). "I loused that up," he admitted. "I really did. I tried to make the heavy, Rod Steiger, understandable as a human being, and Rod did a marvelous job. He became totally understandable, and it threw the whole film out of kilter, because everybody else suddenly became terribly beastly. They hounded him to death, and it was very nasty if you look at it that way. After all, the intention that Rodgers and Hammerstein had was to have a plain old villain in a black moustache at whom everybody could hiss, and I stupidly made him into a human being. It doesn't work. No good."

In *The Day of the Jackal*, however, where the villain is not your everyday bad guy, the realism of characterization added immeasurably to the suspense.

"*The Jackal*," he said, "is my first suspense film since *High Noon* twenty years ago. Actually, I violated my principle not to fall back on old tricks, and I used many things from *High Noon* in *The Jackal*. I had a great time stealing from myself. Technically, the films are similar because of the tremendous fragmentation of scenes in the sense that no

one scene means anything. It makes sense only in terms of what follows and what comes before it. It's the continuity; that's what's important. It's like a piece of music that doesn't have a melody at all and
makes no sense unless it has counterpoint. Each piece of film, in itself,
is perhaps meaningless, but in juxtaposition they become meaningful.
You know, in the most primitive way, let's say I have a shot of a man
swimming and I have another shot of a shark's fin. Each by itself is
nothing, but if you put them together, they build a tension. And that's
the kind of thing that I find very exciting. It's very cinematic, because it
doesn't depend on dialogue all that much. You could forget most of the
dialogue in *The Jackal*, except for the key plot expository lines, and it
would probably be a lot better as a matter of fact." Yet the similarities
between the two films are thematic as well as technical. In both films
there are constant references to clocks as a symbol of irrefutable fate,
and even the plight of the heroes is similar. Both Sheriff Kane and
Inspector Lebel stand alone against overwhelming odds, fighting not
only an enemy but the passivity of allies. Yet this is a theme common
not only to *The Jackal* and *High Noon*, but to almost all of his twenty
feature films.

"The theme of my films is something that concerns me very much.
It's simply a question of conscience if you want to call it that. It is a
question of a person who has strong belief in something and who is
prepared to stand up to it regardless of the consequences. And this can
be expressed in two different ways: either a person in conflict with an
organization, be it the church, the army, or King Henry VIII; or sometimes it is in the conflict within the person himself, as in *High Noon*.
This is the thing I find most interesting of all: something on which you
can do endless variations. You could say that *High Noon* and *A Man for
All Seasons* in a sense is a very similar story. Thomas More and the
Sheriff are cousins in a way."

The idea of the individual standing alone comes from Zinnemann's
own experience. "I was known as the Lone Wolf when I was young, and
I had a hard time getting anywhere because the studios thought I was
non-cooperative. When I started on feature pictures, the material I was
given most of the time was very, very poor. I didn't want any part of it,
so I turned down a few of the assignments and got suspended. This
meant that I did not get paid, and I couldn't work anywhere else until

the film in question was finished by someone else. After that I was known as a troublemaker, and people avoided me. I would literally sit in a big studio for months and no one would talk to me. I was ostracized, that is, until I went off to Europe and made *The Search* in 1948. When I returned, I found—to my amazement—that the film was well liked, and I received a kind of notoriety in Hollywood for a while. The only problem was that people had forgotten who I was and thought I was a new European director who had just arrived from Switzerland. But the real influence on my point of view was again Bob Flaherty. He was a tremendous individualist in the days when that was unheard of. He stood up for his own ideas of picture making against any studio in Hollywood at a time when the studios were run by very tight cliques of autocrats who insisted on having pictures made in their way. It took great courage to stand up against the system, because you could find yourself out of work, and being branded a troublemaker, you would then just cease to function. People like Flaherty were admirable to me, because they had the guts to stand up to that kind of pressure of easy money and refused to make junk or things they didn't believe in."

His next project will again be based on the lone wolf theme. "Actually," he said, "after *The Jackal*, I feel like a lady who has just given birth to an eighteen-pound child, so it's a bit early for me to start thinking about the next one. However, I would be interested in making a film about Abelard and Heloise. I think that love story is one of the greatest tales of all times. Here was this man, Abelard, who was within the church but outside at the same time. He was to the twelfth century what Thomas More was three hundred years later: he was the greatest brain of his century. That film will be tremendously difficult, because it must have a special magic to work. If their relationship isn't magic, then you've wasted your time."

The Day of the Jackal though did not need any special magic to work. "I wanted it to be an entertaining film, that's all. I make my films for myself, really, and hope that the public will like them. The problems have to interest me, and I have to be excited. That's what I hope to transmit to the audience, and that's the way it usually works."

Fred Zinnemann Talking to Gene Phillips

GENE PHILLIPS/1973

I was born and raised in Austria. When I was growing up, I wanted to be a musician, but fortunately I discovered in time that I had no musical talent. Then I tried law and I am not sorry I did, because it taught me a method of thinking. Also, since in Austria in those days canon law was required for law students, I later found that very helpful in making films like *The Nun's Story* and *A Man for All Seasons*. Nevertheless, when I received my Master's Degree in law at the age of twenty in 1927, I felt that I would be bored stiff working in law the rest of my life. So I decided to try a career that would be more adventurous. But when I told my family that I wanted to go into motion pictures, the roof fell in. Motion pictures in those days were not considered to be a serious career. My relatives took turns trying to talk me out of it, coming at me in relays. When I finally persuaded them that I was serious about it, my parents agreed with me that I should go to Paris to a technical school where I could learn to be a cameraman. I attended the Technical School for Cinematography in Paris.

When I finished at the school, I couldn't work in France because I wasn't a citizen, and the political situation in those days was very tight. So I went to Berlin to work as a cameraman. I was fortunate to be the assistant of several good German cameramen. One of them was Lerski, who was perhaps best known as a portrait photographer. He liked to stop down the lens of the motion picture camera in order to get perfect sharpness of focus. This required that he burn a lot of lamps on the set,

Originally published in *Focus on Film* 14 (1973): 23–31. Reprinted by permission of Gene Phillips.

however, and proved very expensive, so he was not often asked to work on a film.

One of the best German cameramen that I ever worked for was Eugene Schuftan, who was later to make several films with Robert Rossen such as *The Hustler*. He was responsible for developing some of the trick photographic effects that were widely used at Ufa, a large studio in Berlin. One trick process involved placing a semi-transparent mirror at a forty-five degree angle in front of the camera lens. This reflected the image of a scale model which was out of camera range and made that image blend with the live action that was being photographed in front of the camera. For example, a peasant might be ploughing a field, with a moving windmill in the background. The turning windmill was supplied by the reflection of a scale model.

One of the films that Schuftan photographed was *Menschen Am Sonntag (People on Sunday)* in 1929. Four non-professionals were selected to play themselves in a film about four young people spending a weekend in the country outside Berlin. I only carried the camera around and measured the focus, but there were some very talented people connected with the film. Besides Schuftan as cameraman, the film was directed by Robert Siodmak and written by Billy Wilder. It was made on a shoestring, and they had to stop every two or three days to raise more money. It was a smash hit and we all thought that we would find it easy to get work as a result.

But just about this time sound pictures were introduced in America with *The Jazz Singer* and *The Singing Fool* and so on. The coming of the sound era took Berlin by storm, and the German industry wasn't prepared for it. Jobs were non-existent, so I went to America to see what sound was all about at first hand. I had wanted to go to America for many years. Like a lot of young people living in the congestion of a big city, I loved to go to Westerns, not so much for the violence, but for the huge vistas and the big sky that they pictured. Hence I was attracted subconsciously to America all along.

Carl Laemmle was the head of Universal Studios at the time, and I had a letter of introduction to him. He probably got dozens of letters of that kind. Nevertheless he was very kind to me when I met him, and he rang his casting director and told him to find me some work. I was hired as an extra on *All Quiet on the Western Front* (1930) and appeared

as a German soldier and as a French ambulance driver. Then I talked
back to the assistant director one day and was fired.

Berthold Viertel, one of the top theatre directors in Germany in the
twenties, had come over to Hollywood to write films for F. W. Murnau
and stayed on to become a director himself. But he needed help with
the technical details of picture making. I got an introduction to him
and persuaded him that I was the man he was looking for. I worked for
him for several years off and on. One evening at Viertel's home I met
Robert Flaherty who had just returned from working with Murnau on
Taboo in the South Seas. Murnau had proved dictatorial and Bob came
back very frustrated. Bob was hoping to make a documentary in Russia.
I admired him tremendously and told him I would be happy to be his
assistant there, since my visa to stay in America was just about up, and
I had to return to Europe.

We met in Berlin in January of 1931. Bob wanted to do a documentary about one of the tribes in Central Asia, but negotiations with the
Russians finally broke down. Bob was a romantic; he wanted the film
to be a monument to a lost culture, whereas the Russians wanted him
to make a propaganda picture showing how miserable these people
had been until the Revolution. Although nothing came of the project,
it was a valuable experience for me. I used to sit and listen to Bob in
these conferences about the film, and by osmosis I gained a whole
point of view about picture-making. Robert Flaherty is probably the
greatest single influence on my work as a film maker, particularly
because he was always his own man. If he believed in a project he
stayed with it, but he was never pompous or self-righteous. He was a
good humored Irishman and a great story teller. But it was impossible
for him to work in Hollywood where you had to know how to bend.
We did some test shots for the Russian documentary, but that was all.
Finally we ran out of money. Bob went to Ireland and made *Man of
Aran*, and I obtained a visa to return to the United States.

That was in mid-1931. I went back to work for Viertel, who was by
then at Paramount. Then in 1932 Arthur Hornblow Jr., the producer,
hired me to work with Busby Berkeley, the dance director, and Gregg
Toland, the cinematographer, on the dance numbers for the Eddie
Cantor film, *The Kid from Spain*. The film was directed by Leo McCarey,
but I hardly ever saw him; my job was on the dance unit. It was a rather

vague assignment. I was to suggest camera angles for the various shots in the dance numbers. The movie was being made by Sam Goldwyn's production company and I remember that working with the Goldwyn Girls was a lot of fun. Choosing the Goldwyn Girls was an annual event. The studio would bring in kids from all over the country, young hopefuls who wanted to get a break in pictures. And some of them did, such as Lucille Ball and Paulette Goddard among others.

After being out of work for a while, I was asked by Paul Strand, the famous photographer, in 1933 to direct a documentary that he had been commissioned to produce and photograph in Mexico. It was eventually called *The Wave* and dealt with the life of fishermen in the Gulf of Vera Cruz. The story concerns a young fisherman persuading the others to form a union and finally being killed for this. The situation is similar to the one that Visconti used in *La Terra Trema*, but *The Wave* was a much more modest venture. It was a sixty minute film which was shot silent. But we spent a year in the jungle making it. That was one of the happiest years of my life. In the jungle one was thrown on one's own resources.

When I returned to Hollywood in 1935 nobody wanted me as an assistant any more and I couldn't get a job directing either. Finally I was hired by the Short Subjects Department at Metro-Goldwyn-Mayer on the strength of *The Wave*. Jack Chertok and Richard Goldstone were in charge of the department, and they were men of intelligence and enormous enthusiasm. The studio used the Short Subjects Department as a workshop to test and train new talent. This was a unique thing in Hollywood—no other studio had such a set-up. From this reservoir of talent the studio chose the writers, directors, and actors who seemed to be the most promising, and promoted them to features. Directors like Jules Dassin, George Sidney, and David Miller got started this way.

You had a comparatively small amount of time and money to make a short. At first I made one reelers, which meant I had to tell a story in no more than 950 feet of film. This meant that one had to develop an economy in story-telling which was good experience. I remember doing the life of Dr. George Washington Carver from the time he was kid-napped by slavetraders as a baby until he was ninety-five in ten minutes. The one reelers were shot silent, because they were narrated. Then

I was promoted to two reelers which used dialogue and were shot as regular sound films.

These shorts had a regular production crew like any feature picture, except that the whole thing had to be shot in six days. You could never use a moving camera because that required too long to light the set. You had to previsualise everything you were going to do in order to make the best possible use of the time you had at your disposal. I had to do a crowd scene outside a hospital at night and was given ten extras for the crowd. So I dressed one of them as a policeman and had him push the crowd back toward the camera. This gave the impression that a great number of people were milling around. Working on a tight schedule and budget forced you to use your imagination; it was a challenge, really, not an obstacle. I did about sixteen shorts, all told.

I was really impressed by the difference between making shorts and features at my first production meeting as a feature director in 1940. Jack Chertok had been promoted from the Short Subjects Department to a producer of features, and he wanted me to direct his first full-length film, *The Kid Glove Killer* (1941) with Marsha Hunt, Lee Bowman, and Van Heflin. Since I had not been allowed to use a dolly on any of my short films, I decided to ask not only for a dolly at the meeting but a crane as well. Nobody batted an eye, except to ask if I wanted a big crane or a medium-sized crane. That made me feel that I had really arrived.

My early features were made on tight schedules and budgets. One had to stick closely to the schedule and the budget unless one had already made enough money for the company on other films to be entitled to a little leeway. Otherwise you were under a considerable amount of pressure. I remember making a picture called *Eyes in the Night* (1942) in which an actor portrayed a blind detective who had a seeing-eye dog. The actor had great difficulty in remembering his lines, and it would take six or seven takes before he would get his dialogue right. The dog, however, was only good for two takes and after that would run and hide. That's the kind of unforeseeable problem you could run into, but you still had to finish on time.

While I was making my first features at MGM, I had the strong feeling of going backwards; it was frustrating to do donkey work, because I felt that I had done my apprenticeship in the Shorts Department. I did get to do one interesting film during that time: *The Seventh Cross* (1944). Perhaps because I knew Europe well, this film about the Second World War seemed to have an authentic look about it and was well received. But after I made it, I ran into trouble with the studio.

I was under a seven-year contract to MGM, which meant that in a sense I was studio property. It is true that the studio had given me the chance to develop and so was justified to some extent in expecting me to cooperate. Nevertheless the contracts in those days were very one-sided. The studio had the option every six months of dropping me, but there were no options on my side. The front office exercised a total kind of power over its employees. There was a kind of jungle telegraph that notified other studios when one studio was having trouble with someone, so that it was difficult for him to get a job anywhere else. Yet it is an oversimplification to say that the studio system was all bad. A lot of good films were made during the era of the big studios, and I grew up and learned my trade in that era.

At any rate, after *The Seventh Cross* I was asked to do a succession of inferior scripts, and I turned them down. I was told by a studio executive that unless I accepted the third one which was offered I would be on suspension. I said that I was terribly sorry but that I couldn't visualise the project; so I became the first director ever to be suspended by the studio. Even though the suspension only lasted three weeks, most of the producers on the lot avoided me afterwards, because I had gotten the reputation for being difficult to deal with. When a Swiss film company who had seen *The Seventh Cross* invited me to come to Switzerland to make *The Search* (1948), MGM was delighted to let me go and agreed to put up the major part of the financing.

The story was about displaced children in Europe after World War Two. Some of the children we used had really been in a concentration camp and others were ordinary Swiss children. For one scene I asked a couple of the latter to look frightened at a woman in uniform, because she was supposed to remind them of the female officers in the camp, and they just looked blank. They didn't know the meaning of fear. Then I told the same thing to two of the kids who had been in a concentration camp and the terror that they registered on their faces was incredible. The boy who played the main part was Czech and he knew German. I tried speaking to him in German, but he wouldn't react to anything I said to him in German, because it reminded him of the camps. So I had to direct him through a Czech interpreter.

Montgomery Clift, who played the American soldier who tries to help the lad, had finished *Red River* before making *The Search*, but it was released after *The Search*. The best compliment that he got for his acting in the film came when someone said to me, "Where did you find a soldier who could act?" He maintained the same authenticity as the children.

My favourite scene is the one in which the boy is afraid of the soldier played by Clift and so Clift opens the door and tells the boy that he can leave any time that he wants to. The boy goes out the door, stands looking back for a while, and then hesitatingly comes back into the house. Here is a human being who has been in a wilderness finally willing to gamble on the fact that this man in uniform is really a decent person.

Without my knowing it, the producers added a narrator at the beginning of the film explaining the postwar background of the story which was really obvious from the images on the screen. It was dubbed in such a way that I couldn't remove the commentary when I found out about it. Otherwise MGM was pleased with the picture, and the bush telegraph sent out the message that I was in the studio's good graces again.

I did one more film under my MGM contract, *Act of Violence* (1949). Then I signed a three-picture contract with Stanley Kramer, who at that time was producing films but not directing. The first of the films that I directed for Kramer was *The Men* (1950) with Marlon Brando, and the second was *High Noon* (1952). *High Noon* is a good example of a team effort. Enormous contributions were made by several people. Carl Foreman expanded the screenplay from a short story and wrote an excellent, detailed script. I was away making a short called *Benjy* to raise money for a children's hospital at the time. Kramer made a big contribution at this stage working with Foreman. Elmo Williams, the editor, shaped the film, and Dimitri Tiomkin, of course, gave the film the excitement of the musical score.

Floyd Crosby photographed the film and had the courage to give it the style that we had agreed upon. Floyd and I thought that *High Noon* should look like a newsreel would have looked if they had had newsreels in those days, and we studied Mathew Brady's photographs of the Civil War as an aid. Up to that time there was almost a religious ritual about the way that Westerns were made. There was always a lovely grey sky with pretty clouds in the background. Instead Crosby used no filters and gave the sky a white, cloudless, burnt-out look. He used flat lighting and that gave the film a grainy quality. From the first day the front office complained about the poor photography. Most cameramen might have struck their colours, but Floyd went ahead anyway. Subliminally the photography created the effect we wanted; it made the film look more real.

I'm told that Howard Hawks has said on various occasions that he made *Rio Bravo* as a kind of answer to *High Noon*, because he didn't believe that a good sheriff would go running around town asking for other people's help to do his job. I'm rather surprised at this kind of thinking. Sheriffs are people and no two people are alike. The story of *High Noon* takes place in the Old West but it is really a story about a man's conflict of conscience. In this sense it is a cousin to *A Man for All Seasons*. In any event, respect for the Western Hero has not been diminished by *High Noon*.

After the release of *High Noon* Stanley Kramer offered me *A Member of the Wedding* in order to finish off my contract. He was going off to Israel to make a picture and designated Edward and Edna Anhalt to write the script and to work as associate producers. Carson McCullers's novel is one of the great works of modern American literature. I remember her saying that loneliness is the great American disease and that is the theme of the story.

The following year I made *From Here to Eternity* (1953), with an excellent script by Daniel Taradash who successfully compressed the novel. The scene that is shown under the credits, for example, is a sort of summary of the first fifty pages of the novel. Montgomery Clift as the hero is seen coming out of the shadows in the background and walking toward the soldiers drilling in the foreground. He has a duffel bag over his shoulder indicating that he is new to the camp. So the theme of the film is implicitly established during the running time of the credits: he is the loner trying to cope with the organisation, symbolised by the soldiers who are going through their drill routine.

Screen adaptations of two stage plays followed: *Oklahoma!* (1955) and *A Hatful of Rain* (1957). I wanted to do *The Nun's Story* next, but no studio was willing to take a chance on it. As one studio executive put it, who wants to see a documentary about how to become a nun? Finally Audrey Hepburn expressed interest in it, and Warners bought the book. I really wanted to photograph the scenes in Europe in a harsh black-and-white and the scenes in the Congo in colour, but I felt that coming back to black-and-white at the end when Sister Luke returns to Europe would be too self-conscious. Instead I tried my best to get the European scenes to look as close to black-and-white as possible. The actresses playing nuns wore pale makeup and I asked them not to wear rouge or lipstick at any time during the weeks that we were shooting the convent scenes in Italy. They complied, but they often had wine at lunch and then would return to the set with ruddy faces.

While Franz Waxman was scoring the picture, I discovered that he had a deep dislike for the Catholic Church and this was coming across in his music. The theme he originally wrote for the convent scenes would have been more appropriate for scenes set in a dungeon. For the final scene, when Sister Luke leaves the convent and returns to the world, he wrote an exultant theme to end the film and I removed it from the soundtrack so that the film ended in silence. He was very upset about this and at the post-mortem after the first preview of the picture he said so to Jack Warner. When Warner asked me about it, I answered his question with another: "What kind of music do you want at the end of the film? If the music expresses gloom it will imply that it is too bad that Sister Luke left the convent. If it is joyful people will think that Warner Brothers is encouraging nuns to leave the convent." And so the film ends in silence, the way I wanted it to.

The theme of *The Nun's Story* (1959) is one that concerns me perhaps more than all others. It has been expressed as follows by Hillel two thousand years ago: "If I am not myself, who will be for me? And if I am only for myself, what am I? And if not now, when?" This seems to me to be a universal theme. It applies to the—sometimes tragic—clash of an individual with the community of which he is a part; an individual who is trying to follow his own, personal conscience against all kinds of odds (*From Here to Eternity* and *The Nun's Story*); it applies equally to a purely interior dilemma, where the conflict of conscience is not directed against an opponent, but rages within the soul of the individual himself (*High Noon, Man for All Seasons*).

Of course this theme is not found in all of my films. The point of *The Sundowners* (1960) for example is that people can be in love even after fifteen years of marriage and can feel secure as long as they are together, even though all they own are the shirts on their backs.

My next film, *Behold a Pale Horse* (1963), was a disappointment. The story, which was about the years following the Spanish Civil War, didn't come across. For example, the film opens with some newsreel footage of the Civil War followed by a scene with Gregory Peck. We duped the negative to make this scene look grainier and grainier so that it blended right in with the newsreel shots. But the sum total didn't come off, and the fact that there are some good things in the film makes it all the more irritating.

Since *Behold a Pale Horse* was a failure, I think Columbia was very generous in letting me make *A Man for All Seasons* (1967). Here was a story with no sex or violence and a great deal of difficult dialogue. One man believed in it among the Columbia executives: Mike Frankovich. Robert Bolt wrote a very disciplined screenplay from his original play. It was his idea to cut out the Common Man who appeared throughout the play. I missed that character since I thought it was a stroke of genius to have him in the play. But having him talk to the audience wouldn't have seemed right on the screen. We were not able to find a way to make it less theatrical.

I began my film career in Germany, worked for many years in America, and am working in Europe at the moment. I think of myself as a Hollywood director, however, not only because I grew up in the American film industry but also because I believe in making films that will entertain a mass audience, not just in making films that will express my personality or ideas. I try to offer an audience something positive in a film, to leave them looking up rather than looking down. When I can manage to do that, and entertain the audience as well, I'm satisfied.

Zinnemann on Working with the Military and *From Here to Eternity*

LAURENCE H. SUID/1974

LAURENCE H. SUID: *Why did you not want to direct* Patton?
FRED ZINNEMANN: At that time I was interested in something else, and I didn't want to delay Frank (McCarthy). That was number one. Number two, I didn't have tremendous sympathy or admiration for Patton as a man, aside from his obvious military genius. At that time, I didn't feel that I wanted to glorify any of the military virtues.

LHS: The Men *is not listed as receiving cooperation. Kramer said it had some help.*
FZ: In my own experience I found that we received enormous cooperation from the Veteran's Administration, which at that time was located in the San Fernando Valley. This was in 1949. Dr. Bors, who was in charge of the paraplegic department, had developed entirely new techniques of treatment only three or four years previously. The facility, the paraplegic wing of the hospital, was still fairly primitive, but the work that was done by the medical staff was truly extraordinary. Almost everyone, patients as well as staff, was very helpful. By that time, many patients had become somewhat adjusted. Accordingly, Marlon Brando was allowed to spend almost three weeks on the ward with a lot of the men, not only to observe them but to really get to know how they felt and what their thoughts were and all that. I felt that the cooperation was enormous but obviously not from the Pentagon, because it wasn't really designed to make the whole business of soldiering very attractive.

Published by permission of Lawrence H. Suid.

LHS: *According to my research, there was a battle at the beginning of the film.*

FZ: There is a brief prologue which is in fact a dramatization of a true happening, of the way in which the leading character, played by Marlon Brando, received his wound. He was on patrol, and having crossed the Rhine, he was shot by a German sniper. He fell but remained conscious for a time. He tried to reached for his gun which was only inches away but found that he could not move. At the time he did not realize, of course, that he was paralyzed.

The whole incident is quite brief in screen time. It was designed to be a sort of foreword to the film. It was shot in the hills and near the studio. The patrol was fairly easy to stage, because there were still a lot of ex-G.I.s around at that time who knew exactly how to behave in this sort of situation.

LHS: From Here to Eternity?

FZ: Harry Cohn, the head of Columbia Studios, bought the book at a time when it seemed impossible that a film like that could be made. For a long time the project was known as "Harry Cohn's Folly."

At the time the book was regarded as a very rebellious piece of writing. In those days, people didn't criticize institutions like the Army too openly. The Army was still very much of a sacred cow, and Joe McCarthy was at the height of his career. It was an act of courage on Cohn's part to have bought the book. He paid the then-unheard-of price of $80,000 for it. Various screen writers tried and failed to organize the material. It took quite a while and several scripts before a then-relatively-unknown young writer, Dan Taradash, volunteered for the job and came up with a marvelous draft, really marvelous.

At that point I was asked to direct the film. The man who ran the show was Harry Cohn. It was his pet project. The producer was Buddy Adler, who later became the head of Fox. Buddy had been an Army officer in the war. It was logical that he would be the man to make the approach to Washington since he had some brother officers there.

To make a long story short, Buddy did get qualified and somewhat reluctant promises of help from the Army who apparently realized that it would be better to do a proper job of it rather than have some fourth-rate picture. An agreement was arrived at. Certain things the

Army objected to, particularly two things. One, the inside of the stockade. The book contained many scenes showing the rough life inside the stockade. The Army said that if that was shown, there would be no cooperation. The second point was the character of the captain, Deborah Kerr's husband, who was ineffectual and a bad officer. The Army wanted to see the man get his comeuppance and be court-martialed or forced to resign. In the book he was promoted to major.

Now the whole point then became: is it worth making that sort of arrangement? I felt that it was. As it turned out, I was sure that it was not necessary to go into gruesome details about the inside of the stockade, because one could see in the escape and the death of Sinatra sufficient proof for what was going on inside and leave room for the audience's imagination.

I personally would have liked to see the captain being promoted, because it was a fine sardonic touch. But it was a sacrifice that had to be made. There were one or two other points which were less important. The rest was just the shooting of it.

LHS: *Could the picture have been made more authentic, more realistic, if shot in the more "liberal" time of the late 1960s? Would the film have been a stronger film?*
FZ: Obviously we could work only within the framework of the period we were living in.

LHS: *The Code Office would seem to have been as much trouble on the film as the military.*
FZ: The Breen Office dealt with non-military aspects. There were some difficulties about it. In the end, we only had to cut very few feet, I think six feet, out of the love scene on the beach. It was quite innocuous, but there it was. I don't think it affected that scene very much.

LHS: *Do you think the changes the military required you to make affected the creativity and the dramatic power of the film?*
FZ: It's not for me to judge. I don't think so. At that time, the film created quite an impact on the audience. Granted the audience of that time was more naive, perhaps more innocent, not used to the kind of shock treatment they get these days.

LHS: *Was there a point beyond which you were not willing to accept changes from the Army?*

FZ: Yes. But that point was never reached.

LHS: *Could you have made the film without help if it had come down to that?*

FZ: No. I would have resigned, because I would not have made it without Army help. I don't think it would have been possible. More specifically, first of all, it was very important to get sharp-looking soldiers who knew what they were doing. If you had done it without Army cooperation, you would have had a bunch of extras who would have done as they pleased. In fact, they would have been a bunch of civilians dressed up to look like soldiers, and nothing would have happened. You would never have had the feeling of tautness, discipline, or any of the other things that were part of the professional American Army.

Secondly, it would have been very difficult to convey the way of thinking, the way of behavior and the various attitudes of these men. Now, mind you, there were not too many scenes where we actually used Army soldiers. There were a few but not very many. But being in the authentic barracks and seeing the Army life around us gave the actors a kind of framework that was very useful for them and helped them create characters who were reasonably accurate.

Thirdly, there was a question of locations. Buddy Adler was able to first of all get the location of the authentic places, Schofield Barrack in Honolulu and Fort Shaffer, both of which appear in the book. Schofield was actually attacked on Pearl Harbor day. We had permission to use a large section of these barracks and to re-create that attack with training planes, of which we had two or three, made to look like a Japanese Zero. All of the equipment was loaned to us and paid for on a rental basis. But the fact that we were able to use it was of enormous value. How else could one duplicate these things?

We were able to rent a lot of vehicles, all kinds of facilities, plus very, very good technical advice. One man who was a tough professional soldier, a sergeant, supervised all the military details, particularly in terms of the main actors, some of whom had never been in the Army. All of those things were so important that without them, to me personally, the film would have been unthinkable. Now, quite possibly, someone else could have done it. But I would not have.

LHS: *You are saying that for your purposes, real live soldiers were crucial to the re-creation of the authenticity?*
FZ: Not just the soldiers alone. All the items I mentioned, all of it put together was important.

LHS: *The technical advisors, did they do more than ensure authenticity? Did they comment on content?*
FZ: They did as they were asked to do. Whenever I had a question, I asked them. If I was satisfied with the answer, I would use it. They were assistants. They didn't make policy in any way, creatively or otherwise.

LHS: *Did they ever say, you can't do this because the Army won't like it, rather than only saying you can't do this, because it is wrong technically or militarily?*
FZ: They had no right to do that and they never did.

LHS: *Only questions of patches, saluting, etc.?*
FZ: Close order drill, formations, everything that goes on in military life; how a barracks is organized, what are the sleeping arrangements, what the mess looks like, all of that, a million details.

LHS: *They insured authenticity?*
FZ: That's all. Yes.

LHS: *Critics suggest they do more.*
FZ: For me a technical advisor has not and never has had any other purpose than to advise on authenticity.

LHS: *Changes in the script were intended to help portray the Army in the best light?*
FZ: There were no basic changes in the script after my arrival. All arrangements with the military were made before I came. I read the first draft screenplay and accepted the assignment.

LHS: *Once the script was done, there were no problems?*

FZ: I worked on the second draft with Taradash; that is the normal pro-
cedure. Once the director goes to work, he makes whatever changes are
necessary from his own point of view. This took a couple of months. I
didn't think any of these changes were even submitted to the Army. I had
nothing to do with that part of it. But I know whatever I finally liked is
what I made. And I was not aware of any further moves by the Pentagon.

LHS: *Were there any problems when the film was sent to Washington for
approval?*

FZ: Not that I know of. I don't think we made any change at all. There
was no censorship attempted even though some people were rather
staggered by Sinatra's death scene and various other things such as the
"treatment," i.e. the punishment Montgomery Clift received for not
compromising. None of that was censored. There was no attempt made
to soften anything of the conflict between Clift, who didn't want to
box, and the officer who was determined to break his spirit. All that
stayed as it was.

LHS: *Because it was a popular book, do you think it was easy to get the story
as it was?*

FZ: That didn't come up. No. At that point, we were on our own. The
book was a frame of reference. But we were making a film. And at a certain point, a novel or a book is a launching pad. A film has a life of its
own, and you have to construct it differently.

LHS: *Did you see the film in the context of an anti-war film?*

FZ: I saw it in the context of what it was about, in terms of the book,
which was the individual striving to maintain his identity in the face of
pressure from a huge organization. Eventually, he goes all the way. The
organization is shown from the worm's eye-view as it were. The soldier
in his inarticulate way says a man has to do what he has to do or something like that. And he does it. He absolutely refuses to be a boxer.
Eventually he gets killed for wanting to be himself. That is really what
it is about. My wish was to stay true to the spirit of the book, which was
not anti-Army. Prewitt is proud to be a good professional soldier, a
thirty-year man. "I love the Army," he says.

LHS: *You were focusing on individuals trying to survive. The Army was simply the environment in which they were functioning?*
FZ: Yes and no. I'm not interested in his trying to survive at all. I was interested in his pursuing his own point of view and sticking to his own convictions come what may, including *not* surviving.

LHS: *The Army and the Department of Defense said they cooperated to "smooth" rough edges.*
FZ: In the two areas I mentioned, they smoothed off the rough edges. I think it's probably a fair description, yes. I regret the captain not being promoted to major. As far as the stockade is concerned, I think in the end I would have done it that way anyhow.

LHS: *Their pressure and involvement except for the promotion/dismissal issue did not affect the way you would have made the film in the context of the fifties?*
FZ: No.

LHS: *Would you have preferred to make the film in the context of the 1960s?*
FZ: Of course not. It never occurred to me to remake a picture I had already made once.

LHS: *Would you want to remake it now, in the new atmosphere of greater freedom?*
FZ: I think it would be quite wrong to remake it. It's a period piece for better or worse. It's got all the limitations of the time in which it was made.

LHS: *The suggestion is that a film is not only about its own subject but contains the period in which it is made.*
FZ: That is not such a new idea, is it? Any film or book or painting reflects the point of view, the thinking and the spirit of the era in which it was made. Could you imagine anyone writing *Madame Bovary* today? Yet it was and still is a great piece of writing. But it's a period piece. It reflects the way people were then.

LHS: *You were in* All Quiet on the Western Front*?*

FZ: It was a marvelous picture. The attitude toward war in that period is reflected in that picture marvelously. It was very, very anti-war just as the book was.

LHS: *It received no help although* Wings *had.*

FZ: No. It was critical of the Army. *The Big Parade* was one of the great, great pictures about war. It's an anti-war picture. It's probably the first great anti-war picture. It's a pacifist film, a marvelous, marvelous film.

LHS: *You did no war films after* From Here to Eternity*? Was that deliberate?*

FZ: In fact there was another picture I made with a war background: *Teresa*. It was a story of a young infantryman with the Italian campaign. He falls in love with an Italian girl and brings her home as a war bride, and the marriage gets into trouble.

We did have Army cooperation in that film from the particular division which fought in that sector, the 91st. It was made in 1950.

LHS: *It's not listed.*

FZ: Perhaps the cooperation came from U.S. Army Headquarters in Europe. Stewart Stern scouted locations and did a lot of preparatory work. We did in fact get some help from the Army including the rental of some old equipment and that kind of thing and particularly the help of a sergeant who had been through the whole crucial battle preceding the breakthrough into the Po Valley and the end of the war.

LHS: *They gave you equipment.*

FZ: We rented some equipment but didn't need all that much. We bought some war surplus stuff on our own. But we got quite a lot of advice. Bill Mauldin was technical advisor. I sold him on the idea of joining us. The sergeant who was also our technical advisor was on active duty. He must have been detached from somewhere. The sergeant was the military advisor and Mauldin was the overall advisor.

Individualism Against Machinery

GORDON GOW / 1976

Remarkably versatile in respect of subject matter, Fred Zinnemann brings to his films a rare combination of efficiency and sensitivity. This is the result, no doubt, of a Hollywood-schooled professionalism that has subtracted nothing from his original European nature. His newest work, *Julia*, deals in recent history and real people: it concerns a dangerous mission undertaken into Nazi Germany before the start of the Second World War by the American playwright Lillian Hellman to aid her friend Julia (the roles are played by Jane Fonda and Vanessa Redgrave).

Based on a story from Lillian Hellman's autobiography, the appeal of this subject for Zinnemann is twofold. "First, I was interested in the relationship between the two women, who were great friends from childhood, and secondly in Lillian's problem when she was put in a situation of great peril and, not being a very courageous person, had to cope with it: that particular problem interested me very much."

Zinnemann's office, where we talked, was scrupulously neat. He chose a straight-backed chair, not on account of one of the back ailments that are so prevalent, but because he had had a slight accident recently while skiing. He is seventy.

He was born in Vienna, and there during his youth he developed his enthusiasm for cinema. "I was studying law at the time, which bored me to death, and rather than go to lectures I went to the movies. It so happened that I saw three or four among those films which really made me believe that being a film director was a creative way to spend one's

Originally published by *Film and Filming* 24, 5 (February 1976): 12–17.

time. They were very diverse. One of them was King Vidor's *The Big Parade*. Another was Carl Dreyer's *Joan of Arc*. A third was Eisenstein's *Battleship Potemkin*."

From such classics of the silent cinema he gained an appreciation of the medium's visual strength. "I found it really an expression of the future which it has become. So many people hardly ever read books any more: they watch the visual medium. It's become a one-sided state of affairs, and that's not a good thing." His continued enthusiasm for words as well as images has been very evident in his films. Music has a deep appeal for him, too, as you would expect of a Viennese.

"I grew up in the Vienna of post–World War One. Almost everybody was either a physician or a musician. My whole family were doctors. My own great interests at that time were girls first, music second, and mountain climbing third. I wanted desperately to be a musician, but I found out that I had a tin ear. I didn't have any talent for it. So simply because I had nowhere else to turn, I went to university as a law student. But music in Vienna is a way of life. There's a saying that if you dial a certain number there on the telephone, they'll give you a note to tune your fiddle; and another thing, which is perfectly true, is that if you see a man walking down the street and everybody stops and takes off their hat to him, there's a strong likelihood that he plays second fiddle in the Vienna Philharmonic. There's that kind of regard for music. Everybody plays something, and in the days after the First World War everybody played chamber music for entertainment, because they couldn't afford to go to the theatre.

"But in those days in professional families the idea of anybody taking up theatrical activities was somewhat suspect, particularly when it came to films. I was suspected by my family of wanting to go into cinema because of girls and the glamorous life. Finally, however, I persuaded them to let me go to a technical school, which was in Paris, and learn the proper technique of becoming a cameraman. I spent a year and a half there, studying the theory and practice of photography and cinematography, after which I was reasonably prepared to be a second cameraman.

"Then I went to Berlin, where I worked for a year as assistant to various cameramen, until everything came to a standstill because very suddenly sound films arrived. *The Jazz Singer* appeared on the screen and silent films were dead. Nobody knew what to do.

"I thought it would be clever to go to America to try to find out more about it. And having done so, I found it so fascinating that I decided to stay; and I spent the rest of my life there, until rather recently when I've lived in England. My intention when I went to the United States was to become a film cameraman, but the unions wouldn't have me, so I was reduced to working as an extra, in which line my first job of any consequence was playing a soldier in *All Quiet on the Western Front*. I was a German soldier and a French ambulance driver, in fact. But after about six weeks I got into an argument with an assistant director, and I was fired.

"After other jobs, though, I was asked by some friends to direct a documentary in Mexico. That was my beginning as a director. The film was called *The Wave*; and on the strength of it I gained a job at MGM directing shorts."

These included several in the *Crime Does Not Pay* series, and the Academy Award winning *That Mothers Might Live* (1938), which was about an Austrian physician who found a cure for child bed fever. "The MGM shorts department was an excellent preparatory school for directors, because we had all the time in the world to prepare a film, but were obliged to shoot it very fast. So we had to be very well prepared—we had to pre-visualise each film. This was meant to teach us that time was money and that the better organised one was the more rapidly one could function. Severe as it seemed at the time, I must say the experience has helped me enormously all my life.

"Now I think the ideal is a mixture of that and the freedom to improvise. I like to pre-visualise a film up to a point, but leave a lot of room for last-minute happenings. I like very much to let things take their course, and to have time enough to incorporate certain things that occur spontaneously. But I do find it necessary to have a sort of skeleton that is very well constructed, and to operate within that framework."

Discipline would appear to have been excessive in respect of the shorts, however. "I remember I had to do one about a Negro scientist, covering the story of his life from the time he was a baby until he reached the age of ninety, and all in ten minutes. Each shot was a

sequence, and we had three days to shoot it in. It's the kind of discipline that can be useful for later on. What's important really is self-
discipline, and I've stuck to that pretty thoroughly all my life."

Early in the 1940s he progressed to feature-length films. One of the
first was *The Seventh Cross* (1944), with Spencer Tracy as a man who
escaped from a Nazi concentration camp. Pre-planning stood
Zinnemann in good stead. "And there was a kind of excitement for a
young budding director like myself in working with a man of the
calibre of Tracy. It's no exaggeration to say that one can learn a
tremendous amount from talented actors. I certainly learned a lot from
him. He had humility. He was an actor in the same sense that Paul
Scofield, let's say, is an actor. He didn't have the pretentiousness of a
star. Once, when somebody asked him how he prepared for a role in a
film, he said, 'I go home and learn the lines.' He was totally unassum-
ing. And there was never a false move about him. Yet he was a very pro-
tean actor, who could change shape and character at will. Fascinating to
watch. At that time there were a lot of young actors under contract at
MGM, and whenever the word went out that Spencer Tracy was going
to do a scene there would be a gallery of the young hopefuls sitting
there watching, spellbound. And the extraordinary thing was that if
you were twenty feet away from Tracy, you couldn't really see or hear
anything very much because he did everything very quietly, yet when
you saw him in the completed film he sort of exploded the screen with
that interior energy of his."

There was a marked difference between the kind of war film represented by *The Seventh Cross* and Zinnemann's later and far more famous
From Here to Eternity (1953) with its sourly dramatic impression of
American army life at the time of Pearl Harbour. Zinnemann empha-
sises, though, that when he made *The Seventh Cross*, "I felt it was very
important to get across the fact that just because you were a German it
didn't mean automatically that you were a monster, which at the time
many people thought was the case—naturally enough, in view of what
was going on. The film was a study of the people whom Tracy met
when he was running for his life, people who were forced by his presence to get off the fence, one way or the other; either they helped him
or they didn't help him. Some took great personal risks; others, who
were old friends, turned their backs and wouldn't have anything to do

with him. It was a very valid study of human characters who were just like everybody else: the fact that they were Germans was purely secondary. That was what was important to me about the picture. Technically it was interesting because it had a very exciting suspenseful construction.

"What interested me most about *From Here to Eternity* was the study of a man who believes in something and is prepared to take the consequences. Private Prewitt, played by Montgomery Clift, was a very fine boxer: a man who had blinded another soldier in a boxing match, and who consequently didn't want to box any more. The whole machinery of the army made efforts to get him to box again, punishing him cruelly, but to no avail, never breaking his spirit. That was what I found important: individual against machinery.

"In a totally different context there was the same thing in *The Nun's Story*: the individual against a huge organisation, following her conscience. Or *A Man for All Seasons*: the man who won't abandon his conscience and eventually pays for it with his life—something that is admirable, and very moving to me personally."

Beyond this recurrent theme in Zinnemann's work, *From Here to Eternity*, showing conditions in the United States Army as far from ideal, and at times downright brutal, amounted to an antimilitary statement that was daring for its period. "There were grave doubts about making the film by people who felt that to defy authority to that extent was unwise. I think the studio showed considerable courage in embarking on the project in the first place."

Nevertheless the army cooperated in the making of it. "That was particularly due to the efforts of the producer Buddy Adler, who had been an officer himself. They only made two conditions. One was that we would not show the environment inside the stockade when Frank Sinatra was a prisoner; and the other was that the captain who was guilty of abusing his authority, who in the novel by James Jones is eventually promoted to major, should in the film be cashiered—made to resign the service. I found it quite necessary to accept. Call it a compromise if you like, but without that I think the film would have been worthless, because I would have been obliged to take a lot of civilians to play soldiers and the whole feeling of the film would have gone out the window."

Among the numerous players in *From Here to Eternity* were Deborah Kerr and Burt Lancaster, she as a frustrated army wife, he as a virile First Sergeant with whom she snatched passionately at temporary release in a love scene that became quite celebrated, raising eyebrows in its day. The pair in swimsuits were engulfed by a heavy surf as they rolled indulgently in the sand. Deborah Kerr in fact, recalled the occasion this year: "We worked so hard, for a whole day. Burt is a very disciplined and hard-working man, and so is Fred Zinnemann. It was wet and gritty and uncomfortable, but we worked and worked, waiting for the right wave. And it was a scene that couldn't be too much rehearsed in advance, because it wasn't determined how we'd do it until we went to the particular beach in Hawaii that Fred Zinnemann had chosen. And then we thought, 'Shall we play it up there, or down here?' And as I remember the idea came quite mutually to play it much nearer the water, so that the sea would roll over us as we kissed."

Locals and tourists gathered inevitably to watch, which didn't faze the surf-swept lovers in the least: "It was a sort of horse-shoe shaped bay, so it wasn't difficult to keep them reasonably well back. But that was done mainly to prevent them making too much noise, so that we could record the necessary dialogue right there and not have to dub. Of course, if you are an actor or an actress, people watching you is part of your job. When you get up on a stage fully clothed, you're stripped naked really. Your emotions and your feelings are up there. You may make a fool of yourself, you may forget your lines, you're truly very vulnerable when you're on the stage. So there isn't that much difference in acting for movies if a whole lot of people are staring at you."

Another Zinnemann film that was essentially concerned with an individual sticking to his guns and following the promptings of his conscience was *High Noon* (1952), a classic among Westerns and arguably the most effective of Gary Cooper's vehicles.

He carried far more strength of character than the usual Western hero, as the Marshal who could find nobody to support him in his stand against some outlaws and was therefore obliged to face them alone—a feat all the more heroic because not only was the opposition seemingly overwhelming but the Marshal was desperately afraid.

That was the aspect that appealed to Zinnemann: "To me the fact that a man is afraid and overcomes his fear shows true courage, whereas a hero without fear, who doesn't know what fear is, basically comes from a fairy tale. He isn't as human as the other kind. Fearless people are beings apart from normal human beings who have normal fears. Surmounting those fears is what makes the situation interesting.

"The divorcement from the traditional Western glamour was carefully planned. I said to the cameraman Floyd Crosby that I would like to shoot the picture so that it would look like a newsreel, supposing there had been newsreels in the 1890s. We studied many photographs of the period. They were very grainy and the lighting was very flat. There were no filters, so the sky was very white. And we tried to accomplish the same thing. We did nothing but front lighting. And above everything else we didn't try to glamourise Cooper. We showed him as a middle-aged man, to which he didn't object.

"The result was that the comparative technical 'imperfection' of it worked for us subliminally. It made the audience feel somehow that the whole thing was more real. This was also the reason why it was done in black and white. I doubt that if we had done it in colour the same thing would have happened. There was a great deal of room for the audience to put their own imagination to work because of the fact that it was black and white.

"I think, incidentally, that if *From Here to Eternity* had been done in colour, it would have looked rather garish, and that would have taken something away from the theme I mentioned. It would have become much more external, and you would be diverted by the beauty of the palm trees and the water."

From Here to Eternity remains the most distinguished of the Zinnemann films that have concerned servicemen, but two earlier ones of note were *The Search* (1948) and *Teresa* (1951), and another of especial interest, in that it marked the film debut of Marlon Brando, was *The Men* (1950). In that case the struggle of the individual was with himself, with his own will. Brando played a paraplegic, a war survivor who was paralysed from the waist down, and who had to overcome his inevitable sense of defeat in order to rebuild himself physically, so that he could make powerful use of the upper part of his body and gradually take his place in the world again.

"That was an inner battle," says Zinnemann. "He was a man obliged to rethink his whole life and come to terms with himself: a man full of energy and vitality, suddenly made a cripple. Credit is due especially to the producer Stanley Kramer and the screenplay writer Carl Foreman, who saw a film in a subject which everybody else at that time considered totally taboo. The documentary element in the completed film did not come particularly from the original setting of the hospital but rather from the fact that we included in the cast a great many actual paraplegics who had been wounded in combat, and those people gave the feeling of authenticity which only an actor of Marlon Brando's calibre was able to equal.

"Marlon, as part of his preparation, spent three weeks in the ward, living with these men, so that not only could he imitate their movements but he understood them very deeply. They became very fond of him. He learnt how to identify with their problems, and this helped him to give an excellent performance."

Something of a departure in Zinnemann's career was *Oklahoma!* (1955), a very lively screen translation of the stage musical, owing much to Agnes de Mille's choreography but nevertheless gaining truly cinematic flourishes from Zinnemann. Especially un-stagey were the opening ride through a field where the corn was literally "as high as an elephant's eye" in accordance with the Hammerstein lyric, and the progress of "The Surrey with the Fringe on Top" as observed by a camera beneath the vehicle, bringing us down to wheel level and demonstrating vividly how "chicks and ducks and geese better scurry" when the cowboy Curly drove in their direction.

Zinnemann himself, however, takes a dim view of his directorial contribution. "It was an experiment on my part, and I think, on the strength of it, that it's just not my cup of tea. Much as I love musicals, I'd rather watch them than make them. I did have a marvellous time making *Oklahoma!*, but thinking back on it I feel I didn't get the best out of the material, and a man who really understands musical comedy could have done better. I'm not trying to be coy: that's the way I feel about it. I was too serious in treating the characters. I made Jud a real human being, and he was not intended to be. He was intended to be a villain with a green moustache, so that when he died everybody was delighted, whereas Rod Steiger played him so realistically that when he finally was killed and everybody rejoiced, it somehow wasn't quite human.

"And stylistically the film broke into two parts: one, the fairy tale figures played by Gordon MacRae and Shirley Jones; and the other the very dark real world of Jud, a man who had a problem, who was a heavy and yet I tried to make him understandable—which I shouldn't have done."

Another adaptation from the live theatre was *A Hatful of Rain* (1957), based on the stage play by Michael Vincente Gazzo, with Don Murray as a morphine addict. "It was a film that didn't go very well. It certainly didn't go nearly as well as Otto Preminger's *The Man with the Golden Arm,* which was made a year or so later and was about heroin addiction."

Perhaps the most remarkable of Zinnemann's films that have been derived from a stage original is *A Man for All Seasons* (1966) for which the playwright Robert Bolt wrote the screenplay himself. Paul Scofield, repeating his original stage role of Sir Thomas More, modulated beautifully under Zinnemann's direction to the more subtle nuances permitted, and indeed required, by the closer range of cinema. The inherent drama of the situation proved as strong in the film medium as it had in the theatre: More, the sixteenth-century statesman who resigned his position as Lord Chancellor of England because of his disagreement on religious grounds with Henry VIII, and who was subsequently imprisoned in the Tower of London and then beheaded, was presented not only as a credible historical figure but also as a man of conscience whose personal agony retained moral significance.

Zinnemann is the first to concede that it was primarily a film of words. "I think there were very few cinematic-type pictures in it. It was a matter chiefly of re-editing the play, transcribing it for film. It depended on magic of the words: that's what it was about in the last analysis. It wasn't cinema in the sense of visual images telling the whole story. One has to accept what's there—the strength that's there, and work from that. If one has a piece of material such as *A Man for All Seasons*, it would be ridiculous to try to superimpose one's own ideas beyond a certain point. What I did was just to window dress it really. I tried to remain true to the substance of the play, which I thought was enormously important. It made life easy for me, because there it was and all I had to do was shoot it."

In spite of which, the spectator at *A Man for All Seasons* in its film version would be remarkably unresponsive if he didn't come away with certain images as well as fine turns of phrase imprinted on his mind. The ritual look of the court, for example, afforded Zinnemann the opportunity for telling compositions of great visual power, as indeed had the convent rituals in *The Nun's Story* (1958), where the inherent drama of the woman prostrate in penitence, her figure severly clad in the black and white habit, prove even more memorable than such overtly cinematic passages of the same work as the location scenes in the Congo. Which is not to say that Zinnemann neglects the intrinsic visual assets of his locations: a keen eye for exteriors informs many of his films, and this is evident not only in the dramatic starkness of the Australian landscapes in *The Sundowners* (1960), but also in the river-scapes that were incidental, but by no means inconsequential, in *A Man for All Seasons*.

A great deal of location work was involved for *The Day of the Jackal*, the suspenseful story of an attempt to assassinate General de Gaulle. But the tension and the topography never got in the way of each other. "It was pretty much a visual kind of project, and very challenging in view of the fact that everybody knew the outcome. As you watch the film, you obviously know that de Gaulle is not going to be killed, and the thing that fascinated me was whether it would be possible, even though the ending was known, to maintain a degree of suspense. A lot of people have said that it came off; others said that it hadn't."

A film of so many different environments, frequently shifting in time and place over a lengthy running time, is a prime example of one of the director's most vital functions: preserving the concept as a whole, making sure that each single facet assumes its proper perspective in the overall scheme that exists, during the shooting, only in the director's mind.

"It's as though you had a basic note in your mind. It's always there—something you have to have. A sustained note. And everything has to harmonise with that along the way. It's like having a compass that points in a certain direction. You have to sense it. You have to know when you are on the beam, and whether you are in danger of going off the beam.

"I'm off the beam very often. I think it's important occasionally to have flops, because one learns a great deal from that. Something else I believe is that one shouldn't compete with oneself, trying always to make a picture that is bigger and better than the one before it. That's a load of nonsense.

"*Julia* is on a smaller scale than *The Day of the Jackal*. It's been very, very challenging, in that it involves two shifts in geography and in time. The film lays partly in America, partly in France and Vienna. But it also takes place partly in 1952, and sometimes in 1925, sometimes in 1934. Negotiating these shifts within the film makes for a technical excitement in itself."

Allied to that, and interwoven with it, is the suspense element of the story, which is very considerable; while a further interrelated aspect, and perhaps the most emotive of all, is the characterisation which once again concerns individuals under stress, calling upon resources of will power in the face of events that seem all too likely to be overwhelming.

Fred Zinnemann and *Julia*

CECILE STARR / 1977

Fifty years ago Fred Zinnemann was a student at the Technical School of Photography and Cinematography in Paris. Now, at the age of seventy one he has just completed eighteen months of work on *Julia*, a movie based on an episode in Lillian Hellman's best-selling book of recollections, *Pentimento*.

In the film, Lillian Hellman (played by Jane Fonda) recalls her struggles to become a successful playwright, with the bemused encouragement of her close friend Dashiell Hammett (Jason Robards), while her best friend from early childhood, Julia (Vanessa Redgrave), has thrown herself whole-heartedly into the fight against the Nazis in Europe in the early 1930s.

In many ways *Julia* is a film that ironically dovetails with Zinnemann's own life. The film journeys from the United States (where Zinnemann made his own successful career as a movie director), to London (where he now lives), to Vienna (where he was born in 1907), to Paris (where he studied film and worked as an assistant cameraman), to Berlin (where with Billy Wilder, Robert Siodmak, Edgar Ullmer, and Eugene Shuftan he collaborated on *People on Sunday*), and on to Russia (where he was supposed to work as Robert Flaherty's assistant on a film that was never made).

Although he turned down many interview requests when he was in New York to help publicize *Julia*, Zinnemann agreed to see me—mainly because we had met twenty years earlier at one of the first Flaherty Seminars organized by Frances and David Flaherty, the filmmaker's widow and brother.

Originally published in *Filmmakers Newsletter* (November 1977): 30–32.

It was Robert Flaherty, he told me right away, who taught him some of the most important lessons he has learned about filmmaking. In fact he still thinks about them. The main thing Flaherty taught him was that a director must never give up his right to make his films the way his instincts and experience tell him they should be made. Since 1957, when he directed *A Hatful of Rain*, Zinnemann has had final say on all his films.

In *Julia* Zinnemann decided to break from the traditional way of filming the important sequences inside the train when Lillian is smuggling money for Julia's underground activities. This would have meant using rear-projection and thus aiming a stationary camera at the area where moving backgrounds would appear. But Zinnemann felt this technique would focus the viewer's attention on the backgrounds rather than on the dramatic tension inside the compartment. So he had the script changed to a predominantly night scene with no backgrounds. In the few daylight shots, he used telephone poles and wires looped for repeated use, running faster or slower as needed. With the mechanical jiggling of the train interior, nothing more was needed to give the illusion of a moving train.

Although he did not say so, Zinnemann probably is also indebted to Flaherty for his affinity to real locations, beautifully depicted, and to the use of non-actors in many of his films. I asked him how he got to be Flaherty's assistant in the first place. They met in Hollywood at the home of Berthold Viertel, Zinnemann told me, after Flaherty's unsuccessful effort to collaborate with F. W. Murnau in the South Pacific. Zinnemann asked Flaherty if he could work with him on his next project. Flaherty told him that if he got himself to Europe when the project was to start, he could have the job. Zinnemann got himself there, and worked with Flaherty for a number of months (without pay, as Flaherty also did). When both had run out of money, Flaherty went to England and Zinnemann returned to Hollywood.

Zinnemann sees *Julia* as a story of conflict inside a young writer who longs for personal success and gradually awakens to social responsibility. And in some ways Zinnemann has lived his own story of conflict along similar lines. There was the lure of Hollywood, epitomized by the success of *From Here to Eternity* in 1956; and there was the wish to maintain his independence and his integrity (he left at least two major productions—*The Old Man and the Sea* and *Hawaii*—because they were not going his way).

Conflict in *Julia* is reinforced throughout the film in its many contrasts of silence and sound, of dark and bright lighting, of loud and subdued colors, of extreme long-shots of natural scenes and extreme close-ups of de-glamorized actors' faces. Zinnemann at first wanted no sound at all during the film's opening credits, but he was advised (and rightly, he feels) that people would think the sound had not been turned on; so, simple drumbeats are used at the beginning followed by a long pause; then loud and unexpected chamber music starts when the title *"Julia"* appears on the screen. The effect is perhaps more startling than the sirens and gunshots that open most movies today.

Julia abounds in visual contrasts as well; Zinnemann feels that in most cases they just happened because they were right for this film. Every film has its own proper elements, he says; what one does successfully in one movie does not necessarily apply to any other. *Julia,* for example, has a number of impressive painterly scenes: the dull grey of a row-boat dimly outlined, where Lillian sits fishing and remembering; the smoke-blue of a train puffing out of a station; the dizzying whiteness of a country snowscape. These shots are almost without motion, distant, beautiful, as one might remember them rather than as they would actually appear. They are perhaps the film's own version of *pentimento*—which Lillian Hellman describes as old paint that has aged on the canvas, becoming transparent and revealing earlier paintings which the artist repented and repainted. These filmic pentimento touches belong to *Julia,* and not to any other film that Zinnemann has directed.

Zinnemann chose the British cinematographer Douglas Slocombe for the filming of *Julia,* mainly because Slocombe's soft-focus camera work had made Katharine Hepburn look half her age in *The Lion in Winter.* *Julia* has many crucial flashbacks in which the two leading women, nearing forty, have to look twenty-two. Not many actresses nearing forty are willing to look their true age onscreen, and in some scenes Vanessa Redgrave looks almost twice her age.

Zinnemann could not praise Redgrave highly enough. He ranks her at the top of a long list of outstanding film performers he has directed— a list that includes Marlon Brando in *The Men,* his first movie role; Gary

Cooper, who won a 1952 Academy Award in *High Noon*; Montgomery Clift, Deborah Kerr, and Burt Lancaster, all Oscar nominees, and Frank Sinatra and Donna Reed, winners, for their roles in *From Here to Eternity* in 1956; and Paul Scofield, another Academy Award winner in *A Man for All Seasons* in 1967. (The last two films also won Best Picture and Best Director awards; and Zinnemann won two other Oscars for earlier short subjects.) Of Vanessa Redgrave he says: She sets the highest goals for herself, and spares herself nothing. Whatever problems she may create simply don't matter. She is more than worth them.

Zinnemann discusses his own films without any apparent ego involvement. He takes his work seriously, and generally he works on serious films. I asked him whether he had sought out films that make some sort of social statement, or whether they simply came to him. The latter has been true most of the time, he told me. But he has lived his life close to and concerned about political and social events. The incident in *Julia* where a crowd in Vienna invade a school and throw a student over a balcony onto a marble floor below is based on an incident he had witnessed and had never been able to forget. This is one detail, among many, that he was able to add to the film because of his own personal experiences and concern.

He sees a young director's first years as an important apprenticeship for learning all facets of filmmaking. Then the maturing director, he feels, should have a chance to try out what he has learned and incorporate it with his own original ideas, with proper supervision and restraint. But the accomplished director, when he's reached professional maturity, should have complete freedom in his work. Young directors today are often restricted by their producers who know very little about production or about public taste. Although Zinnemann has had many disagreements with Hollywood studio heads, he respects their judgment and their knowledge about the business.

The same freedom that Zinnemann wants for himself on a film he also wants for those who work with him. For instance, he leaves the entire first cut of a film entirely to the editor once the rushes have been all screened. It serves two purposes: he gets a rest from the film after the shooting is completed, and the editor gets a chance to show what he sees in the film material. *Julia* kept Zinnemann busy for about six months in the rewriting, casting, budgeting and selection of locations;

four months of filming followed, in England and in France; then another six months of editing, and several months of pre-release activities.

Zinnemann chose Walter Murch as *Julia*'s editor because of his exceptional work on Coppola's *The Conversation*. After screening Murch's first cut of *Julia*, they worked together on the give-and-take editing that is so time-consuming. When the film seemed to be as good as they could get it, Zinnemann was ready to see how the public would react. He relies on previews to help him see what the public accepts—or fails to accept—in his films. After *Julia*'s previews in Toronto and New Haven, twelve minutes were cut out, leaving it at something under two hours in length.

Although Zinnemann lives most of the time in London, he spends several months each year in California because of family ties (his son and grandchild live there), and because he likes California. It was there, in 1930, that he worked as Busby Berkeley's assistant on the dance sequences in *The Kid from Spain*. Then in the mid-1930s, after directing *The Wave* in Mexico, Zinnemann directed MGM short subjects for a number of years—Crime Does Not Pay, Pete Smith Specialties, and John Nesbitt's *Passing Parade*, one of which won him his first Oscar. Then came low-budget features (*The Seventh Cross, Teresa*), and then the big ones (*High Noon, From Here to Eternity*, and so on).

What made him give up studying law, I asked him, to study camera and moviemaking? I loved movies, Zinnemann told me—and those that made the deepest impression were Eisenstein's *Potemkin*, Dreyer's *Passion of Joan of Arc*, Stroheim's *Greed*, and Vidor's *The Big Parade*. More than anything else in the world, Zinnemann said, I wanted to direct movies.

And now, after eighteen months with *Julia*, more than anything else in the world he wanted to get home to London and take a rest—before thinking about directing another movie.

On *Five Days One Summer*

ALAN ARNOLD / 1981

FRED ZINNEMANN: The whole thing started two or three years ago when I went hiking in the area of Pontresina in Switzerland, and suddenly I remembered a short story I had read which had haunted me off and on for many years. It was called "Maiden, Maiden" by the American writer Kay Boyle. The short story itself had a very, very good final solution, or final situation rather, even though the characters themselves were not terribly interesting. But it occurred to me while looking at the glaciers there that this could indeed make a very interesting film, that there was the basis for it there. I also remembered an old legend that I had heard many times in the Alps in various places about a person who had fallen into a crevasse on a glacier and whose body had been discovered many years later perfectly preserved. As luck would have it, I came across a young writer who delivered to me an excellent script. I went back to Pontresina two or three times to find out if it were at all possible to shoot the film there, because to some extent it would interfere with tourist traffic. One would need permissions from the various tourist organizations who would not want to lose tourist trade, but all of that, mainly thanks to Peter Beale, has worked out.

ALAN ARNOLD: *You say the story haunted you for many years. Why, then, did you not film it before now?*
FZ: Because the elements never came together. Though I tried several times, I never found a writer who could write about mountains. You

---

Published by permission of Tim Zinnemann.

have to have done some climbing yourself. Otherwise you really don't know what you're writing about. I wanted to show mountains not merely as backdrops but as characters in the story. . . .

AA: *You know about mountains, because in Austria you were brought up among them.*
FZ: I can't say I did anything particularly spectacular. Lots of hiking and light and easy climbs when I was young. But I loved the feeling one had in those old days of going to a place that was absolutely still, the silence, the feeling of majesty, the mystery of mountains. Climbing had nothing to do with acrobatics then but with moving in a very, very still landscape and fighting the elements. Today's climbing is different, for better or for worse I don't know, but the quality has changed. You have thousands of people doing it, huge amounts of funiculars. Some of the mountains look as though they have spiders' webs all over them with all those cables. An element of haste and pressure has come into it, and the silence has gone to a large extent, except if you go further back into the mountains where there is no tourist traffic. What I'd like to do, without sentimentality or nostalgia, is to try to get the feeling across of what it used to be like. That is why the film is set in the 1930s rather than the present.

AA: *Is it true that at one point you were considering making this movie in black and white?*
FZ: Yes, we did talk about it a lot. The reason was that mountains in many ways are more dramatic when photographed in black and white. Photographed in color they tend to look like whipped cream sometimes, much prettier than they really are, and it takes a special talent to photograph mountains in color; it's not easy. With a man like Rotunno, who is a fantastic cameraman, I feel that it is quite safe to shoot the picture in color.

AA: *Your costume designer Emma Porteous told me that when she was discussing with you what Kate should wear, you again had the feeling there should be nothing very glamourous, nothing very colorful about her clothes.*
FZ: It is very important to maintain the feeling of the period. At that time people wore clothes that were rather subdued in color, very

practical, but nobody worried about looking particularly elegant. In terms of mountain climbing, very colorful clothes came in when the plastic era started with loud blues and reds and greens and yellows. In the old days, the only vivid color you saw was red which was used particularly for crisis situations. There was what was known as an avalanche cord which was red and was about fifty yards long. If you went to an avalanche area, you always let that rope drag behind you. In case you got caught, people could find you.

AA: *When you introduced the 1938 film* The Challenge *the other evening, you said that it was a movie that used mountains not just as backdrops but as characters in the story. Is that what you intend to do?*
FZ: Very much so, because mountains represent individual personalities, you might say. Each mountain is different in character, and I think it's possible to bring that out rather interestingly.

AA: *This is one of the most international of units with people drawn from all parts of Europe speaking their separate languages. This was your choice, but it creates problems too, doesn't it?*
FZ: Yes, it wasn't exactly planned, but I'm very happy it has happened. We've got best possible combination of people, and I don't look at the problems as problems but as a challenge, and I know it's one that will be overcome, because the people get along very well. . . .

AA: *You've never directed Sean Connery before. How is the relationship coming along?*
FZ: I think it's developing very well. He's a fine actor and a nice man, easy to get along with. I'm enjoying it very much.

AA: *Why have you aged him more than his actual years? Was the gap between his age and the girl's not sufficient for you?*
FZ: That's right. I think it's important for the story to make the point that this is a relationship with a man who has passed middle age. Sean is a strapping man in the prime of condition, and I felt that if we gave him white hair, it would help the relationship.

AA: *Have you found all your locations now?*

FZ: Practically, except for a few spots.

AA: *You had difficulty finding the crevasse you wanted, I believe.*

FZ: We went all over the place auditioning crevasses, and we finally found one of the kind we wanted. You wouldn't believe it, but crevasses also have personalities. There are some that are wide and sunny and very friendly-looking, and others which are very deep and narrow and quite dark when you get down, and very eerie, and it's important to know what you're looking for.

AA: *Members of departments tell me that you watch everything, every detail.*

FZ: That's the way I work and have always worked. I think any film is a combination of a million details. The more precisely I look into every detail, the better the final effect.

AA: *Who have you chosen to play Johann, the guide?*

FZ: The boy who is going to play the guide is a young man of about twenty-four who played a small part in *Julia*, the last picture I made. He was then very young and has now developed extremely well. He is a young Frenchman whose name is Lambert Wilson, and he is bilingual. He speaks English without any trace of an accent and doesn't have to think about the language and so can concentrate on a performance. More importantly, he has the curious mixture of great innocence and naivete together with a sort of purity. While he himself is quite an intelligent man and a student, I felt he could play a peasant-guide very well. I think he has a very good future. At the moment he is playing one of the leads in a new production by Jean-Louis Barrault in Paris *L'Amour de l'Amour*. The play is a huge hit, and we had a problem getting him, but it's all working out. What he has to do, the most important thing he has to do, is learn how to climb mountains like a professional. Normally that takes three to four years of very hard work, a very difficult thing to accomplish. He's training like mad.

AA: *Has he had experience of climbing?*

FZ: He has had a little bit but not much, so he has had to start from scratch. As you know, our picture is a period piece set in the 1930s, and the climbing technique in those years was quite different from what it is now, so he has to re-learn. But I am sure he will do very well.

AA: *Did you at any time think of an established player for the role?*

FZ: We did, yes, and there was always something that didn't fit. First of all we wanted someone very young. Also one had to have someone who was a continental and didn't have to do an imitation of a continental, which excluded most English and American actors. Also, he had to be someone who would be very good on a mountain and be a good actor. We were asking for an awful lot. And so, gradually, we found ourselves in difficulties. It was really very lucky we found this man.

AA: *Who drew your attention to him?*

FZ: I would say Margot Capelier, my French casting director, who is a brilliant casting director. She cast him in a bit in *Julia*. He played a young boy in a train who gave a hatbox to Jane Fonda at a very important juncture in the story, and he did it very well. At that time he was very promising, and I saw him once or twice after that.

AA: *Have you seen him in his current play?*

FZ: I didn't have a chance to. He plays Cupid and he's practically naked, dressed in feathers, I understand. It's a very strange play.

AA: *Who have you chosen to play Kate?*

FZ: The girl is Betsy Brantley. As you probably know, we had a huge talent search going here. We looked at a great many of the young students coming out of drama schools. The requirements for the girl were basically that she should be somewhat like a young Maggie Smith, a girl who has a strong personality, who didn't need to be terribly pretty but had to have a great deal of spirit and presence, a sense of humor, and, certainly, self confidence. It was very difficult to find somebody who had sufficient experience as an actress and also enough talent to project that image. Youth was the most important thing, and we went through a great many potentially very hopeful, very interesting young actresses. Betsy seemed by far the best so we took her.

AA: *At one point you were considering Kate Burton?*

FZ: Yes, Kate, I know, has a tremendous future in front of her. She has got a great talent, and she has clearly inherited it. I think she'll be marvelous. It was just that she was a bit young for it, a bit young to take the responsibility of carrying the film, because in the end, the whole thing depends on the girl to an extraordinary degree.

AA: *The picture is set fifty years ago, and the human face changes over the years. Was that a consideration?*

FZ: I don't think it's so much the faces that change as the hair-styles; in the case of men the beards and moustaches. I think faces don't really change all that much. You see a lot of people around today who could well have lived in the Middle Ages, and it's really more the way they present themselves to the world. But, to take your point, Betsy will be entirely of the period after she has been styled for it.

AA: *Do you bring from one picture to another people that you have worked with over the years?*

FZ: I always like to do that if I can. Sometimes it isn't possible. The present group is a combination of people I've worked with for a long time and others who I've never worked with before.

One man in particular is the cameraman who I look forward to working with very, very much. Giuseppe Rotunno has done the last ten of Fellini's pictures and a number of excellent American films, one of which was *All That Jazz*, for which he got the Academy Award. That doesn't necessarily matter, but it is an indication of the quality of his work.

AA: *Who is your designer?*

FZ: The production designer is a Frenchman, Willy Holt, who has worked with me on every picture I've made in the last ten years, although that is only two pictures: *The Day of the Jackal* and *Julia*, the French part of *Julia*, and he's a brilliant architect, and we get along very well. I'm very happy to have him.

AA: *Who else deserves mention at this early stage?*

FZ: I'd like to talk about Peter Beale for a moment. Peter is the executive producer, a young man who has an extraordinary ability of organizing a complicated production such as this, which has difficult locations and a lot of logistics, and he's managed to do that brilliantly with the help of some other people, particularly John Palmer, an old friend who has been production manager on pictures like *Lawrence of Arabia* and *Doctor Zhivago*. The Swiss production manager, Leonhard Gmü, is also first rate. So we are in good hands. And my assistant director, Tony Waye, is a man I worked with on *Julia*, so I know I'll get enormous help in that area.

AA: *How important is Kay Boyle's short story to the content of the film?*

FZ: I have never met Kay Boyle. The rights were obtained through agents. However, she is still a well-known writer and lives, I believe, in San Francisco. I should explain that it was not the characters in the short story that interested me, but the story's final situation of a girl sitting in a hut waiting for two men to come back from a mountain. Only one comes back, but from the distance she doesn't know which one. She knows that an accident must have happened, that one of them may be dead, but she doesn't know which one. She cares about both of them, but she is in love with one of them. That was a good situation. In the story the girl herself seemed very lightweight, the boyfriend, rather oafish, and so there wasn't much else to it. We were in no time in touch with Kay Boyle. The story was bought, and that was the end of it.

AA: *Are you trying to say something in the film about love or marriage?*

FZ: Nothing especially. I just hope that people like it and spend a pleasant hour and a half in the theatre looking at it. I don't like to be pigeonholed as a maker of message films, and there's no theme or characteristic, I feel, common to my films.

AA: *Have your other pictures you have made presented such dauntingly complex logistics as those you face on* Maiden, Maiden *with locations that will take you over glaciers and into crevasses at heights of up to fifteen thousand feet in the Alps?*

FZ: In one way or another several have been pretty tough. One very interesting one was *The Nun's Story*, which we shot partly in Italy and a large part in what was then the Belgian Congo and is now called Zaire. We were there the year before the revolution. A picture that would have been one of the most complex was one I never made. It was canceled at the last moment—*Man's Fate* from the novel by André Malraux called *La Condition Humaine*. Although we would have wished to shoot that in China, which we were not allowed to do at that time, Malraux was helpful in finding us locations in Singapore and Malaysia. We had them all well established when the picture was canceled. *The Day of the Jackal* was complex logistically too, involving constant travel from one place in Europe to another. Logistics invariably are an important element in the process of film making on location.

AA: *You took on a challenge which astonished many people when they really thought about it. How do you feel now that these four months of filming in the Alps are over?*
FZ: When I first started I was naturally terrified by the logistics and the complications of the production. They appeared exceptionally daunting, and the fact that we were to be victims of weather. As you saw, it's impossible to play roulette with nature. You are bound to lose. It's a risk one has to take if one is to make films of this kind. In the overall, I feel from a purely production point of view that it went extremely well. Much, much better than one could have dared to hope, and even if we are somewhat behind schedule, it's rather miraculous that we were able to accomplish what we have, so far as the quantity of the shooting is concerned. As far as the quality is concerned, I think we've got some quite spectacular mountain sequences, particularly the one on the glacier inside the crevasse. Obviously, what the audience will think no one knows.

AA: *What was the tensest moment?*
FZ: It is very difficult to say. One was under constant pressure one way or another. One took things as they came. The tension was constant. The main thing was that the working relations were very good. The crew got along very well in spite of the fact that it was an enormous mixture of languages and nationalities. We had Austrians,

Germans, Swiss, French, Italians, Americans, and British, and somehow they understood one another very well. I recall no unpleasant incident of any kind. The spirit was good.

AA: *I think people felt that if you could get to those high and uncomfortable locations there was no excuse for anyone else not to.*
FZ: Some locations were more difficult than others, of course. The crevasse was particularly complicated and took longer than we thought, and I hope the results will justify the efforts we made.

AA: *Now you have the more dramatic acting scenes to do in controlled conditions.*
FZ: It will certainly help not being a victim of climate as we were in the mountains. I look forward to getting on with it.

Fred Zinnemann: An Interview

MICHAEL BUCKLEY/1983

Fred Zinnemann is a synonym for classicist; his films are synonymous with quality. There's an old world charm about the man, whose first job in Hollywood was as an extra in *All Quiet on the Western Front.* His speech is tinged with reminders of his native Austria, the once curly brown hair has grown sparse and gray; wearing an open-collared dress shirt and gray slacks, his soft voice is tired—not because of age (seventy-five), but the jet lag that has plagued him since arriving four days earlier from his London home. When in New York, Zinnemann always stays at the Pierre: "I have been coming to this hotel since 1953. All the older workers were just kids then. It's fine, as long as the companies pay for it." During the interview, we're interrupted by four phone calls ("See how tough it is to be a director?" he quips) and two deliveries. One bellhop greets him in a thick Brooklyn accent: "Nice ta see ya, Mista Z! Ya here promotin' a new movie?" He assures the director, "Da people dat hire ya, dey know what dere doin'. I know—I go ta da movies!" Returning to his straight-backed chair, Mister Z smiles: "That was quite a nice little testimonial."

The desire to direct was originally instilled by a quartet of pictures: Erich von Stroheim's *Greed,* Sergel Eisenstein's *Potemkin,* King Vidor's *The Big Parade,* and Carl Dreyer's *The Passion of Joan of Arc.* "I decided that here was an interesting medium for self expression." Prior to his decision, he had considered being a violinist ("I'd have ended up in some cafe as third violin") and had studied law: "When I received my master's degree, I felt that I would be bored stiff practicing law the rest

Originally published in *Films in Review* 34, 1 (1983): 25–40.

of my life—so, I decided to try something more adventurous." As a director, his adventures have taken him from Mexico (*The Wave*—the 1937 documentary that marked his debut) to Manhattan (*A Hatful of Rain*—the 1957 feature that was the first on which he had final cut), from the Belgian Congo (*The Nun's Story*) to Australia (*The Sundowners*), *From Here to Eternity*.

"I only learned about acting from actors," claims Zinnemann, who began his career as an assistant cameraman in Paris in 1927. He has guided Montgomery Clift, Marlon Brando, Rod Steiger, and Meryl Streep (among others) through their first screen appearances, and has directed Oscar-winning performances: Gary Cooper (*High Noon*), Frank Sinatra and Donna Reed (*From Here to Eternity*), Paul Scofield (*A Man for All Seasons*), Jason Robards and Vanessa Redgrave (*Julia*). A seven-time Academy Award nominee as Best Director, Zinnemann won in 1953 (*From Here to Eternity*) and 1966 (*A Man for All Seasons*); he's earlier received Oscars for one of the eighteen MGM shorts he directed—*That Mothers Might Live*, 1938—and for his 1951 documentary short, *Benjy*.

With which of his twenty-one features (1942–82), he's asked, do most people identify him? The question adds a new wrinkle to the director's kindly face: "I have no idea. Could you tell me what you think? I'd be quite interested, really." Informed that, for this writer, It's *From Here to Eternity*, his pale blue eyes probe deeper: "That's very interesting. Now, would you say that's because of the main character, played by Monty Clift?" A brief appraisal of the picture precedes a rephrasing of my initial query: "I wanted to know if people, when they meet you, say, 'Oh, yes, *From Here to Eternity*' or 'Oh, yes, *A Man for All Seasons*.'" Replies Zinnemann, "It's very curious. In England, they usually say, 'Oh, yes, *High Noon*.' Perhaps because it's the most popular over there. Of course, it would be unfair to say that I made it—I directed it." (He differentiates between movies which he's *directed*—over which others had the final say—and that he has *made*.)

Though not a commercially successful film, *The Member of the Wedding* (1952) remains the director's personal favorite: "Because it's the one that moved me most deeply—long before I'd worked on it, having seen it on the stage and also having read the original novel by Carson McCullers. The bewilderment and the pathos of the little girl—no longer a child, not yet in puberty, in no man's land emotionally—was heart rending; and, in some funny way, deeply symbolic of mankind. I don't want to sound pompous, but there was something of that. And the way Julie Harris portrayed it, I found totally heart breaking. Also, what I loved about it was it was completely unpretentious, almost like a line drawing; it was a very simple story—without any expenditures— and very, very down to earth."

A Man for All Seasons, however, contains his favorite scene: Sir Thomas More (Paul Scofield) saying goodbye to his wife (Wendy Hiller) and their daughter (Susannah York). "I found that very moving," states Zinnemann. "I remember the editor crying into his moviola every time he made a cut."

His greatest disappointment was the cancellation—"about a week away from production; we'd rehearsed a week or ten days in costume"—of *Man's Fate*. Based on the book by André Malraux ("a marvelous book, my generation worshipped it"), the story of the 1927 repression of Chinese communists by Chiang Kai-shek "had a brilliant script (by Han Suyin) and an extraordinary cast: Peter Finch, Liv Ullmann, David Niven, Max von Sydow." All the sets had been built and over $4 million spent when, in November 1969, James Aubrey, who had just taken over MGM—the third corporate change in as many months—and was seeking to save costs, ended the project. Zinnemann and producer Carlo Ponti sued; and between the "almost three years of preparation" and "a nasty lawsuit," it was "a shattering experience that took four-and-a-half years out of my life."

Life began in Vienna, Austria, on April 29, 1907, as the elder son of Dr. Oskar and Anna Zinnemann, both of whom were later victims of the Holocaust. "I was an only child," he says, "up to the age of thirteen. I have a kid brother, George, who is now a retired colonel in the U.S. Air Force." After convincing his parents that he was serious in seeking a career as a film-maker, they agreed that he should study in Paris. During his eighteen months at the Technical School for Cinematography, he learned the fundamentals of optics, photochemistry, developing and printing. While in Paris, he secured his first professional job, making some shots of machinery for *La Marche des Machines* (1927); and, in Berlin, he worked as an assistant cameraman on three 1929 releases: *Ich Kusse Ihre Hand, Madame, Sprengbagger 1010,* and *Menschen Am Sonntag.*

Wishing to study the new sound technique, young Zinnemann jour-
neyed to Hollywood in 1929, carrying a letter of introduction to the
head of Universal Studios, Carl Laemmle. Not knowing what to do with
him, Laemmle gave the newcomer a job as an extra in *All Quiet on the
Western Front.* "It was very kind of him, because I was totally new and,
that way, I had my first contact in Hollywood." In the classic war story,
Zinnemann doubled as a German soldier and a French ambulance driver:
"Even in that very modest way, I was very, very happy to be part of it."
After three weeks, he was fired for talking back to the assistant director.

Following several months unemployment, Zinnemann became an
assistant to Austrian-born director Berthold Viertel, then under contract to Fox. They worked together on two films: "He had some problems with the language, not too much; but he had a certain amount of
difficulty with camera technique, and, in that sense, I think I helped
him. I also learned a great deal from him, watching how he handled
actors. That was big news to me; I didn't know anything about them."
At Viertel's home, Zinnemann met Robert Flaherty, a pioneer in the
making of documentaries and the man whom he calls "the greatest single influence on my work." The novice asked if he could work with him
on his next project, and Flaherty agreed—providing Zinnemann could
pay his own way to Berlin. They spent six months (without pay)
designing a documentary about a little-known nomadic tribe in a
region of Central Asia that belonged to the U.S.S.R.; but the project was
abandoned due to government interference. "There was a vast difference of opinion as to the approach of the film. Bob was a romantic and
wanted it to be a monument to a lost civilization; the Russians wanted
propaganda. Bob taught me more than anyone else—to concentrate on
subjects I know and to make a film the way I see it."

Zinnemann returned to Hollywood, where Viertel had started directing at Paramount. He assisted him on two Claudette Colbert vehicles,
following which he was hired to aid Busby Berkeley with the camera
setups for the dance numbers in *The Kid from Spain.* Leo McCarey
directed and Gregg Toland (later of *Citizen Kane*) photographed the
1932 musical comedy, which starred Eddie Cantor, Lyda Roberti and
Robert Young. Among the Goldwyn Girls who executed the choreography by Berkeley ("he was a tough taskmaster") were Lucille Ball,
Virginia Bruce, Paulette Goddard and Betty Grable. Zinnemann recalls

it as "a very happy experience—there were fifty beautiful girls, and I was twenty-four or twenty-five at the time."

Another period without work preceded Zinnemann's first chance to direct. "Carlos Chavez, a famous composer, was the head of the Mexican Department of Fine Arts, and he commissioned his friend, Paul Strand, to produce a documentary for his government. My friend, Henwar Rodakiewicz (who supplied the scenario), was supposed to direct it, but he had another commitment and asked me to take it over." *The Wave* featured the native fishermen of Alvarado on the Gulf of Mexico; they played themselves in the story of how they attempted to organize their industry and achieve better working conditions. The Mexican title was *Redes*—"which," explains Zinnemann, "has a double meaning: 'nets' and 'trapped'—which was the situation with the fishermen." *The Wave* "played in art theatres in the United States and became very well known in Europe, particularly in France; and, as I understand it, the Nazis burnt the negative—which was in Paris—so prints are now very hard to come by."

Zinnemann and Henwar Rodakiewicz then co-authored a screenplay, *Bonanza,* which was not produced. "It was eventually sold to MGM. The leading role was that of a young Mexican Indian; and, in those days, one would have cast it with an American actor—perhaps young Henry Fonda—but MGM wanted to do it with Wallace Beery. It never happened."

On October 9, 1936, Zinnemann married Renee Bartlett, who was born in England, raised in Chile, and worked in Paramount's wardrobe department. His bride of forty-six years did not accompany him on his most recent visit to the States. "She's recovering from a knee operation," he explains. Their only child, Tim, is now a producer, of whom his parents are tremendously proud (as they also are of their thirteen-year-old granddaughter, Stephanie). An apprentice to Mike Nichols during the making of *The Day of the Dolphin*, Tim has produced four films: *Straight Time, A Small Circle of Friends, The Long Riders*, and *Tex*. "He also produced the TV movie, *The Jericho Mile*," adds the delighted dad, "and he would very much like to direct, but everything today is a package deal—and he refuses to bow to nepotism."

In 1937, Zinnemann showed two reels of *The Wave* to Jack Chertok, head of MGM's short subjects department, and the producer signed him. As Arthur Knight wrote in the January 1951 issue of *FIR*, Zinnemann stated, "We had quite a group of us—Jules Dassin, George Sidney, Jacques Tourneur, Gunther von Fritsch, Roy Rowland—and it was marvelous training." At first, he made one-reelers, which ran ten minutes and were shot silent, because they were narrated; he later graduated to two-reelers, which used dialogue. In all, he did eighteen shorts during a five year period. The third won an Academy Award as Best Short Subject of 1938: *That Mothers Might Live* was the story of Dr. Ignaz Philipp Semmelweiss, who pioneered in the use of antiseptics in obstetrics. When Chertok was promoted by the studio, he brought Zinnemann, along; thus, the director was assigned his first feature film.

Kid Glove Killer, a Grade B crime melodrama which took place mainly in a police lab, starred Van Heflin (in his first lead), Marsha Hunt and Lee Bowman. "A little crackerjack of a picture," stated the New York *Times* review (4-17-42), "compact and tight as a drum." It continued, "Out of the routine tests of chemicals and spectographs, Mr. Zinnemann has created a good deal of taut suspense." The reviewer complimented Zinnemann for "an expert, straightforward job of directing," and remarking on his background, noted, "It might be a good idea to send some directors of super-colossal specials back to the shorts department to learn a lesson in conciseness." Recalls Zinnemann: "I just remembered that, during the sneak preview, all the executives from MGM got up and walked out in a body. The reason for it was the news had come in that Carole Lombard had crashed in a plane."

Eyes in the Night, which cast Edward Arnold as a blind detective, followed. It was termed "a tidy and tingling little thriller" by the NY *Times* reviewer (10-16-42), who also wrote, "The film has been directed by Fred Zinnemann and produced by Jack Chertok, who earlier proved with *Kid Glove Killer* that a keen imagination can more than fill the gap between a modest budget and a million-dollar allowance. Credit them with a repeat performance." Donna Reed, who eleven years later would win an Oscar under Zinnemann's direction, played against type as Ann Harding's bitchy step-daughter.

The director's first A feature was *The Seventh Cross,* which starred Spencer Tracy, Signe Hasso, Hume Cronyn, Jessica Tandy and Agnes Moorehead. Based on a novel by Anna Seghers, the screenplay by Helen Deutsch was set in a 1936 German concentration camp, from which seven men escape. Crosses are erected, on which each escapee is hanged as he's recaptured; however, Tracy survives and the seventh cross remains unused. Hume Cronyn played an old friend who helps Tracy and received an Oscar nomination as Best Supporting Actor of 1944 (Barry Fitzgerald won for *Going My Way*).

When contacted for this article, Cronyn replied, "In those days, Freddie was insecure. He hadn't made a major picture. And he was stuck with an absolute bastard of a cameraman, Karl Freund, who had done lots of films and didn't make it any easier for him. Jessie (wife Jessica Tandy, who also played his wife in the film) and I took a tremendous shine to Freddie. We'd go, at night, to his office in the shorts department and walk through the next day's shooting—the two of us playing all the parts. In those days, rehearsals were very rare. One of Freddie's greatest assets is his remarkable taste. It was awfully, awfully nice to have worked with him; and one of my regrets is not having done a film with him since." (The Cronyns are currently co-starring on Broadway in *Foxfire*, which he co-authored with Susan Cooper.)

Bosley Crowther, in his NY *Times* review (9-29-44), commented: "Credit Fred Zinnemann, the director, and Karl Freund, the cameraman, for much of the crackling tension and hardpacked realism that prevails." Tracy is said to have remarked, upon completion of the picture, "Watch this young Zinnemann—he's going places." Smiles Zinnemann, "He didn't say it to me." He found Tracy "very stimulating; he was most generous and supportive. We were talking about my learning from actors—I certainly learned a lot from him."

His next assignment was *The Clock*, starring Judy Garland and Robert Walker. Three weeks into production, Zinnemann was told that he had been replaced. According to Gerold Frank's biography, *Judy*, Garland wanted Vincente Minnelli as director. He had just directed her in *Meet Me in St. Louis* and *Ziegfeld Follies*, and she had "fallen deeply in love" with him. She kept her wish a secret until the third week, at which time Minnelli was free to take over. Today, Zinnemann recalls the incident without bitterness: "I think she was probably not getting what she needed from me—in terms of direction. She might have felt insecure working with me. I suppose that it was very important for my education to go through an experience like that. At the time, it was quite a blow."

Things got worse. He directed child star Jackie "Butch" Jenkins in two films, of which he insists "the less said the better." Zinnemann was then placed on suspension for rejecting three scripts in a row. He doesn't recall if it's true that he was the first director ever to be suspended at MGM, but, he says, "At the time, it became quite an event—everybody seemed to treat me as though I'd just got the Purple Heart." It lasted three weeks, following which the search for the right property resulted in *The Search*.

Inspired by Therese Bonney's book of photographs, *Europe's Children*, the first draft of a film dealing with displaced children had been written by Berthold Viertel's son, Peter (who, since 1960, has been married to two-time Zinnemann star, Deborah Kerr). Swiss producer, Lazar Wechsler, who had liked *The Seventh Cross*, asked Zinnemann to direct. Although Viertel withdrew from the project because of script disagreements with Wechsler, he was responsible for introducing Zinnemann to Montgomery Clift.

The young actor had already made Howard Hawks's *Red River*, but that film's release was delayed due to a dispute between Hawks and Howard Hughes involving the similarity of a particular scene to one in *The Outlaw* (on which Hawks had done some work). The sequence in question remained, but the difference wasn't settled until after Clift had appeared on screen in *The Search*.

Clift, with whom Zinnemann would again work in *From Here to Eternity*, became the director's favorite actor. Asked to confirm his quotes concerning the star—"He was terribly sensitive; difficult, but so exciting that it didn't matter" and "He would've made a marvelous director"—Zinnemann replies, "Yes, it's all true." Two of the actor's four Oscar nominations came under Zinnemann's direction; and when Zinnemann won his Academy Award for *Eternity*, he told reporters backstage, "I couldn't have gotten this without Monty."

Interiors for *The Search* were filmed in Zurich; exteriors in Nuremberg, Munich, Frankfort and Wurzburg. The action centered on the relationship between a G.I. (Clift) and the child he befriends. The boy, played by Ivan Jandl (whom Zinnemann chose from a school group in Prague), is reunited at the film's end with his mother, played by diva Jarmila Novotna. Chosen one of the ten best films by the National Board of Review, it was called by Bosley Crowther (NY *Times*,

3-24-48) "a major revelation in our times." To other critics' complaints about the picture's sentimentality. Zinnemann replied: "To show things as they really were would have meant that the American audience would have lost any desire to see it." Without Zinnemann's knowledge, the producer added a totally unnecessary narration at the beginning of the film; he tried to have it erased, but it couldn't be removed without ruining the remainder of the sound track. The picture received Academy Award nominations for Zinnemann and Clift and for its story and its screenplay. Although Clift had written all his own dialogue and several of the scenes, Richard Schweizer (who had rewritten Viertel's script) and David Wechsler (the producer's son who rewrote Schweizer's script) won Oscars for Best Story. An honorary Award went to Jandl for "outstanding juvenile performance."

In an economy drive, MGM had dismissed Zinnemann prior to the release of *The Search,* but quickly rehired him thereafter. *Act of Violence,* his last film under contract to the studio, had the same star as his first feature—Van Heflin; also featured were Robert Ryan, Janet Leigh, Mary Astor and Phyllis Thaxter. Wrote one critic: "*The Search* was real. *Act of Violence* is only realistic." Zinnemann's agent, Abe Lastvogel, advised him not to accept another script he disliked, to wait for something that excited him; and, if necessary, he'd lend him money. For months, Zinnemann rejected offers; he then signed with Stanley Kramer for the producer's third independent picture, *The Men.*

As he had done with *The Search,* Zinnemann used a semi-documentary approach with *The Men,* which dealt with paraplegic American veterans. Filmed on location in the Birmingham Veterans' Hospital, several of the patients played themselves. Winning the leading role over Richard Basehart and "a third actor I can't remember," Marlon Brando made his screen debut as a victim who's initially unable to accept his condition. Brando, who had become a stage star in *A Streetcar Named Desire,* "was a force of nature," according to Zinnemann—"his personality jumped from the screen." The script was written by Carl Foreman and the music by Dimitri Tiomkin, both of whom would work again with Zinnemann on *High Noon.* Selected one of the year's ten best by the NBR, *The Men* was not a commercial success.

Teresa was the story of an Italian war bride who encounters prejudice in New York City from the family of her mother-dominated husband.

Zinnemann directed from a screenplay by Stewart Stern. Pier Angeli had been recommended to Stern by the head of a Rome acting school and had made her debut in Vittorio DeSica's *Tomorrow Is Another Day*. She made one other Italian feature before making her American debut as *Teresa*. John Ericson won the role of the husband over three-hundred other actors at an open audition in New York; and Ralph Meeker and Rod Steiger also made screen debuts in the film. Patricia Collinge and Richard Bishop played Ericson's parents, and Peggy Ann Garner was his sister.

Stewart Stern, whose screenplay for *Teresa* earned an Academy Award nomination, also wrote the script for *Benjy*, which won Zinnemann the 1951 Oscar for Best Documentary Short. Zinnemann says, "I suppose you can't cut an Oscar in pieces, so I got it—but Stewart Stern deserves a tremendous amount of credit. In retrospect, I don't think he received enough."

Zinnemann's second picture for Stanley Kramer followed—the classic western, *High Noon*. "It's actually the work of four men," claims the director, who credits the movie's success to writer Carl Foreman, editor Elmo Williams (Zinnemann left the project prior to editing), composer Dimitri Tiomkin (whose song, "Do Not Forsake Me, Oh My Darlin'," established the mood and was inserted at intervals to add cohesion to the episodic footage), and cinematographer Floyd Crosby. "Floyd and I thought the film should look like a newsreel would have looked if they had newsreels in those days." On his segment (11-8-82) of the PBS TV series, *Word Into Image: Portrait of a Screenwriter*, Foreman claimed, "It's the only time I consciously wrote a polemic. It was my story of a community corrupted by fear—the end of Hollywood. When I was in England (after being blacklisted, which coincided with the start of production on *High Noon*), I was very pleased to get letters from people who said they could see it was about Hollywood. I never said that to anyone. I couldn't even say it to my associates, because then the film would not have been made."

The New York Film Critics selected *High Noon* as Best Picture of 1952 and Zinnemann as Best Director—a parlay not repeated at the Oscar derby. It revitalized the career of Gary Cooper, who won a second Oscar as Best Actor. "Cooper," says Zinnemann, "was at his best when he didn't try to act, when he just was himself instead of trying to be an actor." Nominated for seven Academy Awards, the film won four: Actor, Editing, Scoring and Song.

The Member of the Wedding had a screenplay by Edna and Edward Anhalt, adapted from the play and novel by Carson McCullers. The three Broadway stars repeated their roles. Julie Harris received an Academy Award nomination as Best Actress (losing to another star recreating her stage success—Shirley Booth in *Come Back, Little Sheba*). Contacted for this article, Harris wrote back: "(It) was a very happy experience for me, and it was a pleasure working with Fred Zinnemann. It was wonderful to be reunited with Brandon de Wilde and Ethel Waters and William Hansen, who played Papa. . . . Mr. Zinnemann was very patient and kind." Ethel Waters used to duplicate her stage block- ing, and, if corrected, would say, "My only director is God." Zinnemann laughs, "Somehow, I managed to keep her in camera range."

The Member of the Wedding was the third and last time Zinnemann worked with Stanley Kramer. He refuses to comment on his past quotes concerning the producer (and eventual director): "He wasn't around during *Wedding*" . . . "He told everyone *High Noon* was lousy till it was a smash—and then took credit for it" . . . "He sentimentalized *The Men* by adding Tiomkin's music." Sighs Zinnemann, "It's probably best to let bygones be bygones."

Soon after Harry Cohn purchased film rights to the James Jones best seller, *From Here to Eternity,* it became known as "Cohn's Folly." Several writers, including Jones, failed to adapt the novel. Finally, the task was accomplished by Daniel Taradash. He toned down the sex and sadism, changed a brothel to a bar, and had the offending officer (Captain Holmes, played by Philip Ober) busted rather than promoted, as in the book.

Did Zinnemann, when filming, have any inclination that the love scene on the beach between Burt Lancaster and Deborah Kerr would become so famous? "No," he laughs, "I was too busy to think about it."

The stars of *Eternity,* had plans gone differently, would have been Robert Mitchum as Warden, Aldo Ray as Prewitt, Joan Crawford as Karen Holmes, Eli Wallach as Maggio, and Julie Harris as Alma/Lorene. "Bob Mitchum was considered for the part Burt Lancaster played," says Zinnemann. Cohn wanted Columbia contractee Ray to play Prewitt, but the director insisted that Montgomery Clift be given the role— referring to the character's description in the book as "deceptively slim." He says, "More importantly, it was the story of a man who wouldn't give in, a story about human spirit—and Monty seemed to be the right actor." Had he threatened to quit, if Clift wasn't signed? "I simply said, 'If you want another actor, you'd better get another director.'" (He still feels sorry for the actor who lost out: "Do we have to mention his name?") Crawford didn't play the female lead due to either a dispute over wardrobe or her inability to take second billing to Lancaster; whatever the reason, Zinnemann was very pleased to have Deborah Kerr cast against type. "I thought—if you hear two soldiers saying (of the character) she sleeps with everybody, you look at this woman and you don't believe it. She's a lady. With all due respect, if you looked at Joan Crawford, you wouldn't find it impossible to believe she sleeps with everybody." Eli Wallach had a stage commitment to star in *Camino Real* by Tennessee Williams, and so Frank Sinatra (who campaigned strongly for the role) was signed. "There were no horses' heads involved," claims Zinnemann, making reference to and showing disdain for the famed incident in *The Godfather*. (His regard for Sinatra would seem to have more to do with the other end of the equine anatomy.) "If I hadn't wanted him, he wouldn't have done it." Although Zinnemann states that Donna Reed "surpassed herself," he thinks Julie Harris, who was rejected by Cohn, "would've been marvelous." He sighs, "You can't win them all. After all, I managed to get Monty in."

Asked if it were true that Sinatra had stopped speaking to him because he had sided with Cohn—after promising the actor and Clift that a scene would be shot their way—Zinneman says, "I would have liked to have played it their way; but Cohn, who was very smart, put me in a situation in which I was powerless. He invited a top echelon of Army officers to watch the scene. It was quite possible that production would have been suspended, if they didn't like it. I had promised Monty and Sinatra to do it their way, but I just couldn't do it. It was something that Sinatra couldn't accept. So, he didn't accept it. I'm not sure if he stopped talking to me, or if we just stopped talking to each other; but we did stop talking." Have the years altered the situation? "I have no grudge against him. I think it's a shame he took things so deeply; I can appreciate his reasons. He, I don't believe, understood what a predicament I was in. Quite honestly, if I saw him, I'd say hello. How important can this be? Forgive the expression—it's chicken-shit!"

Claims Zinnemann: "Monty Clift was an inspired actor! He made marvelous contributions. Out of ten suggestions, eight or nine were good. I will go as far as to say he was the basic reason for whatever excellence *Eternity* had." He grimaces at mention of a report that Clift was unable to say the final line during Maggio's death scene, because he was drunk. "I think we are now descending into gossip. I don't believe he was drunk. It was a major fight between Cohn and myself—which he won—over the last line in the scene. After the body (Maggio's) is placed in the jeep, Monty said, 'See that his head don't bump.' Cohn insisted that the line be dropped—and, in those days, I didn't have control."

Zinnemann won the NY Film Critics Award (the second year in a row), the Directors Guild Award and his first Oscar as Best Director. In all, the film received thirteen nominations in twelve categories, out of which it won eight Awards: Picture, Director, Supporting Actor and Actress, Screenplay, Cinematography, Sound, and Editing. "Monty and Burt Lancaster neutralized each other (and William Holden won for *Stalag 17*)," says Zinnemann. Clift, distraught at losing, was given a miniature gold bugle (the instrument he played in the film) mounted like an Oscar by Renee Zinnemann; he treasured the gift the rest of his life.

Oklahoma!, the Rodgers and Hammerstein musical which revolutionized the musical theater, became Zinnemann's only musical. The film starred Gordon MacRae as Curly, introduced Shirley Jones as Laurey, and featured Gloria Grahame as Ado Annie, Gene Nelson as Will Parker, Charlotte Greenwood as Aunt Eller, Eddie Albert as Ali Hakim, and Rod Steiger as Jud Fry. Zinnemann had originally wanted James Dean to play Curly, but that choice was vetoed by Rodgers and Hammerstein. "They chose Gordon MacRae, who could sing." Of Zinnemann, MacRae (also contacted for this article) says, "He's truly an actor's director. What a joy it was to work with him. He deserves any credit or accolades that may be coming his way." Though most Rodgers and Hammerstein musicals were not successfully transformed to the screen, Zinnemann blames himself for *Oklahoma!*: "I tried to humanize it, and that was my fatal mistake. I failed to bring *Oklahoma!* to the screen with the kind of purity it had on stage." Bosley Crowther disagreed: "It magnifies and strengthens all the charm that it had upon the stage." (NY *Times*, 10-11-55).

The first film on which Zinnemann had final cut was *A Hatful of Rain*. Based on Michael V. Gazzo's play, the picture starred Eva Marie Saint,

Don Murray, and Anthony Franciosa (nominated as Best Actor) in the roles originated on stage by Shelley Winters, Ben Gazzara, and Franciosa. It was the first movie to depict drug addiction after the Production Code was revised to make treatment of the subject permissible.

Zinnemann spent four months in Cuba working on *The Old Man and the Sea*, but finally informed producer Leland Hayward that he couldn't continue. "That was not a happy experience, for many reasons. First of all, the material was not cinematic. It was a wonderful piece of prose in its own right, but anything that one added to it only took away from it. (John Sturges eventually directed Spencer Tracy in the film.)

The Nun's Story won Zinnemann his third Award as Best Director from the NY Film Critics, which also voted Audrey Hepburn Best Actress. He was chosen Best Director by the NBR, which selected the picture as one of 1959's ten best. Though nominated for eight Oscars, the film won none. (Patricia Bosworth, who later wrote the better of two biographies on Montgomery Clift, was ninth-billed as Simone.)

Also voted one of the NBR's ten best was Zinnemann's next film, *The Sundowners*. (They chose Robert Mitchum as Best Actor—for *The Sundowners* and *Home from the Hill*.) The NY Film Critics selected Deborah Kerr Best Actress; and though nominated for five Academy Awards, the picture failed to win any.

Zinnemann was supposed to direct *Hawaii* (eventually done by George Roy Hill), but left due to script difficulties; he also spent time preparing *Custer*, which was later directed by Robert Siodmak. Other projects on which he's labored were *The French Lieutenant's Woman* (directed by Karel Reisz) and *Abelard and Heloise* (never produced). "I *have* worked consistently," he explained, "but many of my projects died during the embryonic stages."

Behold a Pale Horse was not a success. Wrote Bosley Crowther in the NY *Times* (8-14-64): "It is a shame that a film made as beautifully as *Behold a Pale Horse* . . . should be short on dramatic substance and emotional urgency." From failure, Zinnemann bounced back with a huge success. *A Man for All Seasons* won him his fourth Award from the NY Film Critics, which also chose it as Best Picture and Paul Scofield as Best Actor. He won his second Award from the Directors Guild (which, in 1970, would select him—for his body of work—as recipient of their highest honor, their D. W. Griffith Award). The NBR also chose him as

Best Director, and picked Scofield as Best Actor, and Robert Shaw as Best Supporting Actor. (The film was one of their ten best). Nominated for eight Oscars, it won six: Picture, Director, Actor, Screenplay, Cinematography, and Costume Design. Wrote Bosley Crowther (12-13-66): "Mr. Zinnemann has crystallized the essence of this drama in such pictorial terms as to render even its abstractions vibrant."

It was seven years later that Zinnemann's next picture reached the screen. *The Day of the Jackal,* based on the best seller by Frederick Forsyth, was a success. Four more years passed before *Julia*. It was originally scheduled to be directed by Sydney Pollack, but he was delayed with *Bobby Deerfield*. Based on an episode in Lillian Hellman's 1975 autobiography, *Pentimento,* the screenplay was by Alvin Sargent (who won an Oscar). Jane Fonda starred as Lillian Hellman; Vanessa Redgrave and Jason Robards won Oscars for their Supporting performances. (Maximilian Schell was chosen Best Supporting Actor by the NY Film Critics.) Meryl Streep made her first screen appearance; and the film received eleven Academy Award nominations.

Five Days One Summer (1982), the latest Zinnemann film, stars Sean Connery and two newcomers: Betsy Brantley and Lambert Wilson. The latter had a bit part in *Julia* (as the messenger at the railroad station who delivers a hatbox to Jane Fonda) and was described by *Variety* as having "something of the young beauty of Montgomery Clift." Zinnemann agrees, "He definitely has that kind of charm." The film did not enjoy the best of reviews.

The motif for most of Zinnemann's movies has been a search for self-image: "I have always been concerned with the problem of the individual who struggles to preserve personal integrity and self-respect." Representations of this include Marshal Will Kane, Robert E. Lee Prewitt, Sister Luke, Paddy Carmody, Sir Thomas More, and Lillian Hellman. What is Zinnemann's self-image? "I'm a Hollywood director, who wants to please a mass audience. I don't believe in selling personal beliefs—just in making good movies."

Sir Richard Attenborough, discussing *Gandhi* in the *NY Times* (11-28-82), said, "It is the narrative filmmakers who I most enjoy. D. W. Griffith is among those who influenced me most. I don't think I have ever been disappointed with a Fred Zinnemann picture."

Dialogue on Film: Fred Zinnemann

AMERICAN FILM INSTITUTE/1986

Fred Zinnemann has won four Academy Awards for directing: for two short documentaries, *That Mothers Might Live* (1938) and *Benjy* (1951), and for two features, *From Here to Eternity* (1953) and *A Man for All Seasons* (1966). He was also nominated by the Academy for Best Director for *The Search* (1948), *High Noon* (1952), *The Nun's Story* (1959), *The Sundowners* (1960), and *Julia* (1977). The New York Film Critics Circle has honored him four times for Best Direction; the Directors Guild of America presented him with two awards, and in 1970 conferred on him the D. W. Griffith Award for lifelong achievement in film.

These accolades have been heaped on the shoulders of a man who has been called a "maverick director," whose concerns have been with maintaining his independence and integrity, who took the advice of his former agent (Abe Lastvogel) when he said: "Don't take anything you don't want to do, and if you run out of money, I'll help you." This is a director who has consistently refused to pander to the viewer, whose films "invite the audience to use their imaginations."

Zinnemann was born in Vienna in 1907, studied and worked in Europe, and counts among his early influences such classics as Eisenstein's *Potemkin*, Dreyer's *The Passion of Joan of Arc*, Stroheim's *Greed*, and Vidor's *The Big Parade*. He worked on the famous semidocumentary *Menschen Am Sonntag* with Robert Siodmak, Edgar Ulmer, and Billy Wilder. On moving to Hollywood in 1929, he entered the film

Originally published in *American Film* (January–February 1986): 12–13, 62, 66–67. © 1986 American Film Institute. Reprinted by permission of the American Film Institute.

industry as Berthold Viertel's assistant, and later collaborated on documentaries with Robert Flaherty and Paul Strand. When in 1937 he moved into shorts and later into feature production at MGM, his background in "social realist" documentary style was still evident in his major works, now acclaimed for their authenticity and historical reconstruction. Although his films have occasionally been dismissed by some in the industry as too depressing or too highbrow, audiences do not seem to object to his rigorous moral stance and antiromantic approach. Zinnemann sees his work in a wider context than most Hollywood filmmakers: "One of the crucial things today [is] trying to preserve our civilization."

QUESTION: *Please tell us about your start in film and how you got from Vienna to Hollywood.*
FRED ZINNEMANN: Actually, I'm a disappointed musician, but very early in life, I discovered that I had a tin ear, so that was the end of the dream. Yet I did find out later on that there is in fact a good deal of similarity between a conductor and a director, in the sense that you work with a large number of people. What you have to do is persuade them of your own vision so that they form one body working together for one purpose: to get the ideal result.

But I found all this out much later. In Vienna, shortly after World War I, there was no such thing as a film industry, except for two or three small companies. I studied at a technical school for cinematography in Paris, which proved to be excellent experience, because one learned all aspects of filmmaking.

I was working in Berlin when sound films came in. Suddenly films like *The Jazz Singer, Singing Fool*, those first Warner Bros. films, arrived in Europe, and silent films—regrettably—came to a standstill. And I decided—I thought it a really clever idea—to go to America and find out more about sound and then come back to Europe.

Well, when I got here, I was spellbound, so I stayed. My first job was due to an introduction to the head of Universal, Carl Laemmle, who was known as "Quiet Uncle Carl," a very, very nice gentleman who had no idea what to do with me, and turned me over to a casting director, who said, "We're just making a war picture here, *All Quiet on the Western Front*. Have you been in the German army?" And I said, "No." And he said, "It doesn't matter." So I became an extra, and I played a German soldier and a French ambulance driver for about six weeks.

But the most important thing in my own view was my meeting with Robert Flaherty, who inspired me, not only as a filmmaker, but as a man, primarily because he was a person who never made any compromises, no matter what. He probably made no more than about six films. I admired the way he went about it enormously.

I worked with him for six months in Berlin, mostly testing cameras for a film he wanted to make about a little-known tribe in Central Asia. The negotiations went on with the Russians for about six months. In the end, it came to nothing. By that time, Bob was out of money and so was I. In spite of that, just sitting with him and drinking beer by the gallon, I got by osmosis a small part of the spirit of this extraordinary man.

I then got a job in Hollywood in the shorts department at MGM. This was a very interesting experience, because I saw the entire studio system from the worm's-eye view, as you can imagine. At the same time, I learned a tremendous amount, particularly in terms of discipline, self-discipline. The idea was you were hired at an extremely low salary. You were given a script that you could accept or turn down. You could work as long as you wanted on it to prepare it. But you had to prepare it to such a point that you could shoot one reel in three days, or if it was a two-reeler, you could do it in six days—no more. There was also the discipline of not having more than $15,000 to a reel, of which $5,000 was overhead, and of telling a story concisely, in ten and a half minutes, because one had only 950 feet of film to play with, no matter what the story. They would say, "Here's a scene. There's a hospital in an American city, and it's burning. It's night and there's a crowd watching it. For the crowd, you get ten people." What do you do?

So that, more or less, was the way I started. The studio system—there are two sides to it. A lot of people feel, quite rightly, that it was oppressive in many ways, that the bureaucracy was enormous. On the other hand, it did give you a chance to learn your profession in a continuous manner, without having to fight for a job from one film to the next.

QUESTION: *Many of your films seem to deal with social issues. Could you elaborate on your philosophy as a filmmaker in terms of the kinds of stories you choose?*

ZINNEMANN: I don't have any preconceived ideas about it except that I know my limitations. I wouldn't try to do high comedy, because I don't have the sense of timing, and I don't believe I should try to do musicals. I just like to do films that are positive in the sense that they deal with the dignity of human beings and have something to say about oppression, not necessarily in the political way but in a human way. I have to feel that what I'm trying to do is worthwhile.

QUESTION: *What were your considerations in choosing* Julia?
ZINNEMANN: Several things: One was the story of the friendship of the two women. The other was the fact of conscience—the fact that a woman who is leading a comfortable life is suddenly faced with the question of life or death and decides to go ahead and risk taking the money into Germany. I always find questions of conscience very photogenic. That kind of interior drama is to me very, very exciting because, among other things, I feel that the fact that somebody shoots a gun is of no interest. What I want to know is why he shoots it and what the consequences are. Which means that external action as such is less important than the inner motive through which you get to know what the person's about.

QUESTION: *Performances in* Julia *were just marvelously modulated, very impressive. What was your experience in working with these actors?*
ZINNEMANN: All I had to do with Vanessa [Redgrave], and this was the second time I'd worked with her, was have an hour's conversation about the character, in my office. (I like to talk to each actor separately, individually, and in-depth, so that they understand the whole development of the character—the relationships.) And after that we hardly ever talked on the set. She just went ahead and did it and she was so good that I used to forget to say "cut," because I felt I was a spectator. Jane [Fonda] works in a different way. She has a marvelous quality—she can cry at will in quantity. She can give you buckets or drops and whenever you want it. She is really fantastic, but with a totally different approach, and it was utterly fascinating to see those two women together.

QUESTION: *Do you do a lot of research for your films?*
ZINNEMANN: It depends very much on what kind of a picture you're dealing with and what sort of story you're telling. Some films don't

need it. For *A Man for All Seasons*, the only research you could do was read a few of the historical books; the rest of it came from the marvelous play by Robert Bolt. But on *The Nun's Story* we did a year's research. It was a difficult subject—the Catholic Church was very cautious at first about doing a film where a professed nun left the convent after seventeen years. They said that this was open to being sensationalized and they also worried about an implied love affair with the doctor. It took a lot before they would trust us. I'll give you a very quick example of the kinds of discussions held on the script. There's a scene when the young girls are first coming into the convent, as postulants, and the mother superior explains to them that the life of a nun is a life against nature and the monsignor who was in charge said, "You can't say that. You have to say. 'The life of a nun is a life *above* nature.' " On that one word they spent about four hours of very learned theological discussion. It went back and forth, and finally a Jesuit came and said, "Well, why don't you say, '*In many ways* it's a life *against* nature.' "

It was all a challenge. The whole thing is that one has to approach it not as a problem but as a challenge, and see how you can get around it and what you can do about it. It's surprising how often you succeed.

One of the things I wanted to do on the film was not to have any Catholics, not the writer or the actors, because I was worried about getting an "in" film—a film that would be very meaningful to Catholics but that nobody else would want to look at. So in order to make the actors understand the rhythm and what happens at a convent, we got permission to put each one of them, separately, into various convents in Paris. This was in January, when it's very, very cold and convents are the coldest places in Paris.

We stashed out eight of the leading "nuns" in different convents, and I made the rounds every day in a taxi from one place to the other to see how they were getting on. They had to get up at 4:30 A.M. and go through the entire day, and then in the evening they had what was called the "grand silence"—after a certain hour you don't talk any more until the morning. They had to go through all that, and it helped them enormously in playing the parts.

QUESTION: *Can you pick out some of the films you've made that you've been particularly pleased with?*

ZINNEMANN: I feel very happy about *High Noon*, which was a com-
bined effort. For the visual concept, the cameraman, Floyd Crosby, and
I started with the idea that we wanted to show a film set in 1880 that
would look like a newsreel—if there had been newsreels and cameras in
those days. And in order to do that, we studied photographs, particularly those of Mathew Brady, who was in the Civil War, and noticed the
flatness, the coarse grain, and the white sky. So we deliberately set out
to re-create that. The tradition in Westerns at that time was to have a
pretty, filtered gray sky with pretty clouds and be theatrical about it. I
wanted to have a newsreel quality to give the thing a reality. No filters.
This is also why I didn't want to do it in color.

My whole idea in shaping the drama of the film was to play the
threat as statically as possible—a sort of "organpoint" hanging over the
action. But I also wanted to confine the whole thing just to the village
itself. And show the menace, the threat, only in a static shot of the
rails, the railroad tracks, as against the constant motion of the man
who is looking for help—Cooper (always dressed in black)—against the
white sky.

The third part of the visual pattern I used were the clocks, increasing
in size as the urgency grew and as time kept slipping by, pendulums
moving more slowly, the whole thing finally settling into an unreal sort
of suspended animation, familiar to those who have been faced with
sudden death. (The clocks were of course part of my original pattern
indicated on the pages of my shooting script, which is now in the archives
of the Academy of Motion Picture Arts and Sciences in Beverly Hills.)

It's a picture about conscience. It's not a Western, as far as I'm concerned; it just happens to be set in the Old West. It has to do with a
man who is about to run away, and then stops and says, "I can't do it.
I've got to go back." And when he's asked why, he says, "I don't know,"
and then goes back, and takes the consequences, right up to the end.

QUESTION: *Do you get involved with choosing actors? How about Marlon
Brando in* The Men?
ZINNEMANN: The wonderful thing about that film was that Stanley
Kramer, Carl Foreman, and I were our own front office. We didn't have
to bargain with anybody or persuade anybody. I remember Kramer

bringing up three possibilities, and Brando was one of them. We all felt that Brando would be the most interesting. He had just finished *A Streetcar Named Desire* on-stage, and it was just a question of how he would work out, not having ever worked in film.

QUESTION: *Did he have some of the same problems that many stage actors do when they move to film, of projecting too much?*
ZINNEMANN: You know, it's a totally individual thing. Some actors adapt almost immediately, without any problems and others have great difficulty. Brando—it was not easy for him. On the other hand, once he got the knack, he was tremendous.

QUESTION: *So he wasn't hard to direct?*
ZINNEMANN: No. But one can't really talk in those terms, because it's not like being a schoolteacher. I think people with that kind of talent are entitled to have some elbow-room, because their instinctive talent is such that one would be really stupid not to take advantage of it and see what they're going to do. If you feel that you need some correction or balancing or whatever, then you must discuss it.

Of course, the director has the job of getting the right person for the right part, and that usually means not to cast on the nose. In other words, if you succeed in casting against type, you usually reveal hidden facets of an actor's character. Take Deborah Kerr in *From Here to Eternity*, who up to that point had played the Virgin Queen of England and was seen as a very cold, remote sort of person. Early in the film, one soldier says that she sleeps with everybody on the post. This would have been very flat if we had had a very sexy actress playing that part, because people would have said, "Well, OK, so what else is new?" In the case of Deborah, they were really intrigued, because they couldn't believe that this very ladylike person would sleep around with a lot of enlisted men, and this created quite a bit of genuine suspense.

QUESTION: *What's your opinion of the kind of pictures studios are turning out now?*
ZINNEMANN: The studios by and large are run by people who don't know anything about show business, because they're primarily moneymen.

Whereas in the old days the studio heads were people who had enormous practical experience and were showmen.

That is what's missing to a great extent today in the upper echelons. But more important and more dangerous, I think, is the uniformity of stuff that's coming out. Our only defense is, I think, to remember the standards of our forefathers and the kinds of pictures they made.

A Hollywood Legend's List

DAVID GRITTEN/1993

If anyone should know the ingredients for an Oscar-winning movie, Fred Zinnemann is that man.

The veteran director, one of film history's most distinguished names, brought twenty-odd pictures to the screen in a career spanning forty years. Marlon Brando's debut film was Zinnemann's *The Men* (1950). Montgomery Clift won an Oscar in Zinnemann's *The Search* (1948), his first major film role. Meryl Streep's screen debut was in Zinnemann's *Julia* (1977). Five Zinnemann films—*The Search*, *High Noon* (1952), *From Here to Eternity* (1953), *A Man for All Seasons* (1966) and *Julia*—captured a staggering twenty-five Academy Awards among them.

Zinnemann, eighty-five, quit filmmaking ten years ago, but given his astonishing track record, he seems the ideal man to cast an eye over this year's major Oscar contenders.

Zinnemann, who has lived in London for thirty years, still watches films, enthusiastically if selectively. Because he has a hearing problem, it is difficult for him to view films in a crowded theater; instead he watches them on video in his central London office.

At the request of *The Times*, he saw six films—*The Crying Game*, *A Few Good Men*, *Howards End*, *The Player*, *Scent of a Woman* and *Unforgiven*—which are nominated either in the best film or best director categories.

Originally published in the *Los Angeles Times*, 28 March 1993: 4, 86. Copyright, 1993, Los Angeles Times. Reprinted by permission.

In assessing each, Zinnemann commented on several aspects of movie-making: directing, acting (including supporting roles), casting, cinematography—and in one case, stunts. He started on a note of caution about the tendency of today's movies to be gore-soaked or to dwell on society's psychopaths:

"I've always felt drama at its best should be a mix of terror and pity. Of pictures today, many are long on terror, and either short on pity or without pity at all. Many movies share with TV a hypnotic and addictive element which can rob you gradually of a sense of reality and judgment, and which can actually change the way you think. That is, they can make you follow and accept the ideas and values of other people. I'm sick of sick movies that deal with rage and hatred, of which violence is the daughter."

The Crying Game

"I was tremendously impressed with *The Crying Game*. Looking at it, you felt both the terror and the pity—not only in the splendid performance of Stephen Rea, which was extraordinary, but also of Forest Whitaker. Rea makes a lot of fancy leading men look one-dimensional and flat. He has great depths of compassion; you feel he is a victim as much as [Whitaker].

"I feel one small negative thing: The film ends in melodrama shortly after the IRA people come back and find Rea. This gets to be very plotty and turns into a kind of contrived ending. Miranda Richardson is marvelous, but she enjoys playing a villain too much and it shows; it makes the situation even less probable.

"I saw Neil Jordan's *Mona Lisa*, and liked it. This is a man who knows about pain and suffering. There were some fine supporting performances in *The Crying Game*: the bartender [Jim Broadbent] for one, the leading terrorist [Adrian Dunbar] another. The stuntmen were marvelous. The twist in the story certainly surprised me.

"The film has something of the spirit of [Irish playwright] Sean O'Casey. It also reminded me of John Ford's film *The Informer*, because it's about people who are victims of their own characters.

"I'm very high on this movie."

A Few Good Men

"*A Few Good Men* is one of the few pictures that give me hope that there's still a future for movies and that we are not reduced to a diet of robots, rage and hatred.

"There were two outstanding performances here: an excellent one from Jack Nicholson and a very good one by Wolfgang Bodison [as the young African-American lance corporal defendant]. [Bodison] played it from the heart and gut. I've never seen anyone express contempt with just one look the way he does. He was enormously good at conveying complicated emotions without a word. You knew exactly how he felt.

"Tom Cruise is one of the really excellent young stars in movies; he's very promising. I find some of his mannerisms similar to Montgomery Clift, the way he spreads his hands when he makes a point. He's not at Clift's level yet; but perhaps he's young, and hasn't suffered very much!

"It was directed brilliantly by Rob Reiner, just the way a commercially successful picture should be. It was well organized and well told. The production's perfect, but it was not overproduced; you didn't feel they were trying to stun you with effects. It all seemed to blend properly; if you come out of a movie and say, 'Wasn't the music great?' you know that movie's not in balance. This wasn't like those films where you're supposed to be stunned by the money poured into them.

"People have said Demi Moore's role was redundant, but from the audience's point of view it was important to have that emotional conflict, which you don't have without a woman character who is more than just a [cipher]. The tension between her and Cruise in the beginning makes the audience respond much more than if it was a straight documentary. He's so glib at first, he's insufferable.

"All the stuff about how great Cruise's father was—that's sophisticated subterfuge. You could pull the story apart, but who wants to? It's a good picture and deserves to be shown. It's not a picture you come out of and feel ashamed to be a member of the human race."

Howards End

"As for *Howards End*, unfortunately, there's little good I can say. It's overproduced, and it deals with people who don't seem to be really human in the way they behave. I've seen it twice but couldn't identify with it.

"From the technical point of view, it was brilliant. The trouble was I found myself admiring the set, the set dressing, and the costumes—but not the people. It's like some old MGM movies before World War II, which tried to impress you with their tremendous luxury.

"It's terribly dated. Take *Upstairs Downstairs* [the Masterpiece Theatre series on TV], which was of the same period; some of those people were characters you could really respond to. I found it hard to get interested in what Emma Thompson or Helena Bonham Carter were up to. The only emotion was a detached feeling of saying how well made it was.

"With *The Crying Game*, it was just the opposite. It didn't look as good in terms of costumes, for instance, but that took nothing away from it. *Howards End* is a rich-looking film, as opposed to one made by people who had to make do with spirit and talent.

"I'm not a fan of Emma Thompson. As for Vanessa Redgrave [an Oscar winner in Zinnemann's *Julia*], I know her well and I know what she's capable of. I don't think she was very good in this. She has wonderful technique, but knowing her the way I do . . . I wanted to believe her and I didn't.

"You win or lose a picture on casting at the end of the day. Either I believe an actor or I don't. I cast Edward Fox in *The Day of the Jackal* because he was believable. He had to say a ridiculous line—'Nothing is ever a lady's fault.' But you believed him when he said it, and that was good enough. John Huston worked the same way—he felt the right combination of actors is what makes a picture."

The Player

"I thought *The Player* was a brilliant documentary about Hollywood. It's depressing to think how true it is. My wife saw it with me and was extremely depressed too. I didn't find it at all funny! Maybe that was because I don't find any exaggeration in it.

"Robert Altman's a brilliant director; he's an innovator. The script and direction here are first class. Technically it was wonderful. I love the long opening shot. *Nashville* was a revelation to me at the time, and I think Altman's a great master. It's wonderful how he has kept his independence from the powers that be, creatively speaking.

"In every way it's a first-rate job, and it's wonderful to see it nominated [for best director and in two other categories]. It was hard to find pity for most of the characters in the picture, but that's not what it was about."

Scent of a Woman

"I have very little to say about *Scent of a Woman*; I'm surprised it was nominated. I didn't like it at all, though I thought the boy [Chris O'Donnell] did nice work. I thought Al Pacino was miscast; this was a self-indulgent performance. I simply didn't believe a lieutenant colonel would behave like this character.

"As for the story, I thought it went to great lengths to prove a point, but again, I didn't believe it. This was a movie that didn't know when to stop; it seemed to me there were about four separate endings."

Unforgiven

"*Unforgiven* is a marvelous movie, though it's too long on terror, not long on pity. By *terror*, of course, I mean violence. It's enough to kick a man in the head twice; you don't need to show him being kicked the whole length of Main Street.

"I admire a lot of things about it: Clint Eastwood's direction, the acting, the whole production. It might have been shorter, but that's not important. It's an excellent, outstanding film which deserved to be nominated. Some things about it are really spectacular. Gene Hackman is wonderful; he has a real feeling for the visual mood of a film.

"Clint has managed to make the Western alive and credible as opposed to some of the phony jobs that have been done. In the best sense of the word it was authentic; people moved and talked in an authentic way.

"I've liked some of Clint's work in the past. As an actor he's not versatile, but what he does he does extremely well. He's a positive part of our profession. Some people, you're embarrassed to be in the same business with them. Some movies belong in psychiatrists' closed conferences rather than movie theaters. They're not entertainment in any way."

Zinnemann, an academy member, would not disclose which way he would cast his votes, though he readily conceded that "Neil Jordan and Rob Reiner are enormous talents."

"I'm amazed and delighted by the success of *The Crying Game*, which is a classic story of someone running around scratching up money while they're shooting," he added. "That's how some of the best pictures are made. They share a kind of purity; they don't seem influenced by the rules and regulations of corporations. I have particular sympathy because I've tried in my own work to be as independent as I can, though I was influenced by Hollywood in my formative years; it's something you can't get rid of.

"These movies have made me feel optimistic about film, even if I'm pessimistic about attitudes at the top [of the studios]. The only important question these days is the bottom line. It doesn't matter if someone eats his own grandmother in the movie. This is an attitude that's terribly destructive.

"All these filmmakers have an uphill battle against that kind of attitude. So many people in movies today have no respect and don't know very much about films. In my day, people were greedy, sure, but they loved movies. You could have a professional respect for them."

Conversation with Fred Zinnemann

ARTHUR NOLLETTI JR./1993

This interview took place in two forty-five- to sixty-minute sessions at Fred Zinnemann's office in London on March 17 and 18, 1993. A warm and gracious man, Zinnemann did his best to accommodate me and to answer whatever questions I asked. He even made sure that we sat close together, so that we could have a genuine conversation. The only thing between us was a lamp and small table. The interview begins with Zinnemann himself setting the scene.

ZINNEMANN: Well, first of all, I'd like to say that whatever I talk about is, from the point of view of today, obsolete because the values I grew up with no longer exist to any great extent. But I'll say what I have to say. Now, concerning the position of a film director: in my day the film director was, ideally, the only man who had the central vision of a film. By that I mean he was the one person who, once he had a script to his liking, could really visualize what he was after, what kind of actors would be best for the action, how the picture should look, how it should sound, and what sort of pace it should have. And this would then be tested at a preview to see if the audience went along with it. After that, he had the right to recut or change the film. When it came out, it was that man's picture. It was John Ford's *Stagecoach* or Billy Wilder's *Sunset Boulevard*. It did not matter to the public whether it was

Originally published in *Film Criticism* 18–19 (Spring–Fall 1994): 7–29. The slightly modified version reprinted here was published in *The Films of Fred Zinnemann: Critical Perspectives,* edited by Arthur Nolletti Jr. (Albany: State University of New York Press, 1999): 11–35. Reprinted by permission of *Film Criticism.*

a Fox movie or a Paramount movie. Ideally this was the way a director functioned.

Producers, if they were very good, were not only immensely helpful but also usually came up with the original idea, so that they had a function which was secondary to the function of a director and the making of a film. John Ford would not have a producer tell him how to shoot a picture, what kind of set-ups to use, or what kind of actors to use. Creatively, he was the locomotive. There were a number of us who worked like that. Granted, there were many others who weren't so fortunate. And that was based, I think, primarily on box office and secondarily on the caliber and quality of the pictures. There were of course a number of excellent creative producers. And you know the names as well as I do, so I don't need to go into that.

Anyway, to me being a director is comparable to being a chef in a restaurant. Let's say you have a chef who is famous for making a very good soup, and he has associates who supply the various ingredients. The writer invents the recipe, and so forth; but the director is still the only one who creates the soup from the recipe, who brings it to reality. (The French word for "director" is *réalisateur*.) The producer is the owner of the restaurant.

The other people are each authors of their own thing. In other words, the writer is certainly the author of the screenplay, the cameraman is the author of the photography. But all in all, the author of the *film* is the director, the only person who has the *central*, over-all vision of it from beginning to end.

It is very regrettable that today in an era of mass production the producing arm has become so strong that a film is now judged only by the bottom line: how much money does it make? And if it makes one hundred million dollars, it's a better picture than if it makes fifty million dollars. It's twice as good. This did not necessarily hold true in my day because producers were showmen. They were very good businessmen, but primarily they were showmen. They were excited about the idea of making an audience feel good, because it was the obvious way to make big money at the boxoffice. Today that doesn't matter. You can torture an audience, and if they pay their money, it's still a great picture. On the other hand, today's audiences obviously enjoy being tortured and pay for the privilege. I find this a bit sick. And usually these pictures are wonderfully well made; it's just they are very cold, most of them.

NOLLETTI: *That's because they aren't much interested in humanistic values, unlike your films, Ford's or Wilder's.*
z: That's right. Well, I'd just like to make that very clear because a lot of the things that I may be talking about don't apply any more.

N: *I want to hear whatever you have to say. So do the readers.*
z: Well then, I'll go on. . . . I'll continue because I also would like to say [something about] the great difference between the producers of those days and now. If you take Sam Goldwyn—you may have heard this story about him. He was producing a picture that he liked very much, and he said, "I don't give a damn if it makes a nickel, but I want everybody in America to see it." Nowadays it's not that at all. It's a very different kind of business.

And the way most of us [directors] went—subconsciously, I think— was [to follow] the two-thousand-year-old rule that a drama, in order to create real emotional relief, has to have a balance of terror and pity. Today, a great many of the films have a lot of terror but very little pity, or no pity at all. And that's why I say they are cold as stone, so many of them. Well, I think I've given you the introduction to how I see this thing.

N: *Let's start with some general questions. As you know, proponents of the auteur theory have been highly critical of your work. They say that you maintain a safe middle distance from your material because you don't want to get too involved with it or with your characters. How do you respond to this?*
z: Of course I'm involved with my characters. Ask most actors who have worked with me. Ask Vanessa Redgrave. The "safe middle distance" is nonsense. It's just that I don't like to put people under a microscope and look at them as if they were like so many bugs. As to the *auteur* theory: it has always seemed to me to be little more than a gimmick, creating a completely arbitrary and pedantic set of rules by trying to put everyone's work into "artistically correct" pigeonholes. As Billy Wilder once said to me, people should be judged by the best work they have done. The rest is a sort of sterile bureaucracy.

N: *In fact, to pick up on a related point, you've always been interested in allowing audiences to make up their own minds.*

Z: Of course. Rather than pushing things down the audiences' throats, I strongly believe in allowing them to use their own imagination.

N: *Like the ending of* The Nun's Story *[1959] where you fought not to have Franz Waxman's music—*

Z: Yes—

N: *—because you felt it imposed an interpretation.*

Z: That's right.

N: *Don't you think that allowing an audience to make up their minds can actually be a way for a director to express his personality?*

Z: I wouldn't know, because I don't think in those terms. All I think about is that when I'm very moved by something and very excited about it, I would like to share it and express it in the only way I can. It's that simple.

N: *It's been said that your films have a common theme, the struggle of the individual.*

Z: Well, it's not, you know—Perhaps I should say this: I work by intuition, by instinct, not by analysis. All I worry about is, Am I moved by the story emotionally, or am I not? If it's just cold logic, if I don't find something in it that is inspiring or exciting, something that makes you feel that the human spirit still exists, then it's not for me. You see? So that's the only way I can go. I can't say I'm doing this because the theme is a noble theme or anything. But I can say that [in *A Man for All Seasons* (1966)] Thomas More standing up for what he believes in, until he gets his head cut off—which in his defeat is really a victory—is to me a celebration of the human spirit. I also feel that this is something that we have been missing a great deal [recently]. There are some films—well, offhand, for instance, *Dead Poet's Society*. I think it's a great picture. *Breaker Morant* is also a great picture. Those are the kind of pictures that leave you with some belief in the human spirit,

and you don't feel ashamed to be a member of the human race when
you leave the theater.

N: *Let's talk about your visual style, how you formulate the visual plan for
your films—like, for example,* High Noon *[1952].*
z: Well, that's purely intuitive, you see. It so happens that my
imagination starts with the visual end of it so that, after reading the
script [for *High Noon*], the first thing I saw in my head were the railroad
tracks pointing to the horizon, [which] never allow the audience to see
beyond the horizon, except to know that whatever bad news comes, it
would come from there. Then it occurred to me that it would be interesting to see *in contrast* the marshal [Gary Cooper] moving about all the
time. So we had a static main theme and a dynamic second theme. And
that was then accentuated by the urgency of time—the clocks—which
gave a strong and growing feeling of time being your enemy. So that's
how the visuals came to exist. When it came to what the story was
about, as you probably know, it seems to mean different things to different people. To me, it was a simple thing. To me, it's a picture of conscience as against compromise: how far one can follow one's conscience
before having to compromise—just that, nothing else. That's universal
theme, and never mind whether it's an allegory on the Korean war, as
an *auteur* critic wrote.

N: *In terms of your preparation, how extensively do you story-board?*
z: I just do thumbnail sketches. In the book [Zinnemann's autobiog-
raphy] which you've probably seen, there is a page full of little thumbnail sketches just outlining the action. I normally don't do that
anymore. It's just a memorandum for myself, nothing else. Sometimes I
explain it to the art director because it looks like a hieroglyph . . . primitive and hard to decipher.

N: *One thing that amused me in your book was how John Ford, after seeing
your first film, told you to quit moving the camera so much. Did you take
that advice to heart?*
z: Very much, very much. I think it's something that Ford had his
own reasons for, but when you look back, you can't necessarily go

along with it. Ford said to me that he liked to treat the camera like an information booth, meaning that he would move the characters in such a way that when he wanted them in close-up, they would actually be moving into a close-up. Well, I think it's brilliant. And I do feel that if you move the camera there has to be a reason beyond just trying to be brilliant. I don't think you should ever in a film have people be conscious of how brilliant the direction is. If people come out of a film and say, "Wasn't the music good?" or "Wasn't the photography great?" it means that the film is not in balance because all these things have to be blended, like soup, in such a way that there's not too much salt in it, there's not too much pepper in it, and that you're not even aware of which is what; you're just aware that it tastes good.

N: *Your moving camera, though, is never just functional. It dramatically heightens emotional feelings.*
Z: Yes.

N: *Two examples come to mind: in* The Member of the Wedding *[1952] the camera moving toward Brandon de Wilde's room the night he is dying, then pulling back from it on what turns out to be a morning weeks later. And in* The Nun's Story, *the tracking shot from the train that is taking Audrey Hepburn away from her beloved Congo. The moving camera here is—*
Z: Very important.

N: *Which brings me to another characteristic of your work: the finely toned, often understated, emotional quality—as in the scene in* Julia *[1977] when she [Vanessa Redgrave] and Lillian [Jane Fonda] meet in the Berlin cafe. How do you know the exact tone that a scene should have emotionally? How do you get that tone?*
Z: That's a very interesting question. That is part of a director's preparation, because you have to visualize a scene, you have to get a feeling of what it is that you want to accomplish. And one of the things I knew was that the scene was played in a public place, so there couldn't be a lot of visible emotion. They would try to guard themselves as far as they could so that people wouldn't pay attention. That was number one. And they [Vanessa Redgrave and Jane Fonda] were both very aware of it, because we talked about that. The other thing is that Vanessa is

one of the great actresses of the century; she has a brilliant talent of not appearing to be acting. She's just there, just like Spencer Tracy, and so that when she says a line that could be terribly emotional like, "I had a baby," she eats caviar and sounds very casual about it. She plays away from the line, you see. Vanessa is the kind of actress that doesn't need to be told things like that.

N: *Also, she's perfectly cast.*
z: First of all, in casting perhaps the most important thing I have to help me is that I have a good instinct for talent. I can spot a talented actor; I can spot the actor who has a facet in his or her character that has not been seen in pictures before, like Deborah [Kerr] in *From Here to Eternity* [1953], where we actually cast against type. And it's very interesting because it has to do with applied psychology, really. So once I find the kind of people that I sense can do the job, provided that they are talented actors, or uninhibited nonactors, we sit down, we talk about the character, talk about how it develops, talk about the relationships, and I tell them how I see it. I don't tell them how to do it, because I'm not an actor myself. A man like Kazan, who was an actor himself, can talk to actors almost like a teacher, which I can't do. Nor do I feel I need to. All I do is use my instinct for casting and let the actors feel that I trust them and have respect for them, and encourage them. And then that makes them very free to do things which they normally perhaps wouldn't do. And it's a very happy kind of work. And so I get along with talented people. If by some chance I get a mediocre actor, I get very frustrated.

N: *Getting back to the scene in* Julia, *one reason it's so effective is that while Redgrave holds herself back, Fonda does a lot of crying.*
z: Yes.

N: *Were you surprised to see her do that?*
z: [*Laughs*] No, of course not. Jane is technically superb. She can cry on demand and in the quantity you want. She can cry a drop or a bucket on cue, depending. It was an actor's performance, and a very, very good one. I was not surprised, of course not, because I knew what was going to happen. But I was pleased to see how well she and Vanessa

did it. As a director, you have a sense of what you want. Let's call it 100 percent. Now if you get 80 percent, you are in good shape. If you get 90 percent, it's very good. If you get 100 percent, it's quite rare. But these two were 120 percent, way beyond what I thought could be accomplished. They shared a triumph, I thought.

N: *While writing your autobiography, you must have gone back and looked at your films, some that you hadn't seen for awhile.*
Z: Yes.

N: *Had any of your impressions or opinions changed? Were you surprised by what you saw in any of your films?*
Z: Not really, no. I can't say I had much emotion one way or another. Occasionally I thought, "It's pretty good." There were a couple which I hated that I had to do because of the contract, the two Butch Jenkins's pictures, *My Brother Talks to Horses* [1947] and *The Army Brat* (*Little Mister Jim* [1947]). And before I knew how to defend myself, I got in a position where I had to make these two pictures. So I learned my lessons through that.

N: *Speaking of lessons, in your book you say that you didn't feel you were in command as a director until* Act of Violence *in 1949. That is almost fifteen years into your career.*
Z: Well, I was underplaying it a bit. I knew a few things, but that was probably the first time I really felt comfortable knowing exactly what I wanted and exactly how to get it. But I can't tell you why really. One of the reasons was that the actors were so good, Robert Ryan and Van Heflin. And Janet Leigh was marvelous; it was one of her first pictures. Also, I thought the story was good. I liked the story; I liked the picture. And I felt that my visual imagination was getting liberated more and more.

N: *How so?*
Z: Well, for instance, one of the earliest shots is a shot of Robert Ryan, who is walking, trying to cross the street. A band comes by with the American flag, and then he keeps walking and goes into a hotel. It was all done in one shot. I got a kick out of that, because it wasn't an easy

thing to do. And I liked the idea of this man, who was a victim of an inhuman experience in war [he was a prisoner in a German concentration camp], having to step back because a few old guys were walking past him carrying the American flag as though they owned it. There was an irony about that that I liked, although I don't think it was picked up by too many people. There are certain things you like to do for your own pleasure, and some people catch them and others don't— like the judge in *High Noon*, who talks about compromise and at the same time is folding the American flag and sticking it in his pocket. Working the flag the way he does is what makes the scene interesting.

N: *Plus, it's ironic that after telling Gary Cooper he doesn't have time to give him a civics lesson, that's exactly what he does.*
z: Yes, yes. The same thing happens later. Another character comes in [to Cooper's office] and is very enthusiastic about joining the posse, but comes back later and finds that he's the only person. And at that point he says, "Well, I'm on your side," and as he says it, he plops down his star, and then he starts backing away and all that. I like touches like that. I like in *High Noon* the shot where Cooper finally comes out of the office and goes up the street all by himself—the boom shot. It gives you a lot of fun. So, in other words, I like individual little spots that give me pleasure, but I can't say that this picture is better than others. As far as I'm concerned, *Member of the Wedding* is very moving because of the actors' performances. I think they [Julie Harris, Ethel Waters, and Brandon de Wilde] are all marvelous, and there was not very much work needed, because they had done this play for two years and were very well rehearsed.

N: *Many of your films deal with the subject of medicine. Is this a special interest of yours, or has it some relationship to the fact that your father was a doctor?*
z: Probably. But it just sort of happened. I did that short subject on child bed fever [*That Mothers Might Live* (1938)]. With that one having got the Academy Award, I seemed to be the specialist for "doctor's pictures," which pleased me. I enjoyed it. That sort of led to a series of other films about doctors. . . . [W]e did what I thought was a good one on insulin [*They Live Again* (1938)], one on sleeping sickness [*Tracking*

the Sleeping Death (1938)], and then two or three others. It was always interesting. And then when I did *The Men* [1950], which had to do with a doctor and a group of paraplegic war veterans, that was because Carl Foreman and Stanley Kramer asked me to direct the film. And I was delighted. At that time the executives at any big studio would have dropped dead if you had come up with a subject like that.

N: *I've also noticed that your films are very interested in process, how something is done—for example, the different stages involved in becoming a nun, the step-by-step working out of the assassination plot in* The Day of the Jackal *[1973], and so on. Is this interest related to your work or training in documentary films?*

z: I never thought about it in that way. The thing is, I always like to know why something happened, why so-and-so says this, or why he reacts like that. *Why* is a very, very important word in my dictionary. So "why" is probably the answer to the question you are asking.

N: *In other words, a natural curiosity.*

z: Yes. With *Day of the Jackal*, in the book a part of the excitement [had to do with] the fact of how the gun was put together. The idea that excited me was to make a suspense film where everybody knew the end—that de Gaulle was not killed. In spite of knowing the end, would the audience sit still? And it turned out that they did, just as the readers of the book did.

N: *That left you free to concentrate on another level of suspense.*

z: What was also interesting was the ironic point that one person could bring the entire country to a stop. The entire government, the entire army, the entire air force—everything stopped dead. And they still couldn't find him [the "Jackal"] [Edward Fox]. Then his whole plot went wrong; it got wiped out at the last instant because de Gaulle bent too far forward [during the formal ceremony] to kiss a soldier who was very short. I thought it was interesting.

N: *And ironic, too. Plus, the authorities never learn the Jackal's true identity. There's also another nice irony, which you talk about in your book,*

regarding Cyril Cusak, the gunsmith. For him, the entire matter is strictly a
business transaction.

z: It's very sinister actually, particularly because Cusak looks sort of
bland, you know—a very nice gentleman, a serious businessman, an
engineer. Nothing wrong with him. It made me think of our atomic
scientists and others.

N: *Yes, that idea comes across. You're really making a sly point here about*
the absence of moral responsibility.

z: Even when he [the gunsmith] asks if it's going to be a head shot
[instead of a chest shot].

N: *Nobody ever thinks of Fred Zinnemann as being a director of suspense*
films, yet that is what a good number of your films basically are, like The
Day of the Jackal, The Seventh Cross *[1944]*—

z: And *Act of Violence.* Well, I don't know why that happened. It probably has to do with pigeonholing. You know, many critics just look at
one thing, and they become full of preconceived notions and dismiss
everything that doesn't fit in. So that all they seemed to know about
me was that I was hammering away at integrity, which is nonsense.

N: *It's certainly too narrow a view of your films, because you have other*
concerns, too.

z: Yes.

N: *Since leaving MGM, you've worked as an independent, yet in a previous*
interview you called yourself a Hollywood director. What did you mean by
this?

z: Yes. What I meant was that [although] I have been independent of
major studios since 1948, I learned my trade in Hollywood first in the
very tough school of short subjects and then [during] the seven years of
being an MGM staff director under contract, and in theory having to
accept anything they asked me to shoot, [which was] where I got into
trouble. But I did learn my lessons there. And I learned how to organize
my thinking, and I learned how to tell a story, or at least I hope I
learned—up to a point anyway. Because in short subjects, having ten
minutes to tell a story on a subject like, let's say, Dr. Carver, the black

scientist, from the cradle to when he was ninety—telling it all in ten minutes was quite a challenge! So you learned economy in the best sense of the word. You learned that you had to get your point across in a minimal amount of time to make the maximum impact. And that training in itself was of incredible value.

N: *You learned your craft, and you learned it well. Do you ever feel, however, that when people say, "Fred Zinnemann is a superb craftsman," the word* craftsman *is almost like a left-handed compliment?*
Z: Yes, I do, I do. I think there's more to making films than just the craft, because technique is nothing but an instrument. You know, I come from Austria where music is a very important way of life, and they have a tremendous, tremendous respect for musicians, like good violin players. But they don't have much use for a virtuoso. In other words, if there's a violin player whose technique is terrific, and he can do very difficult things, but musically he hasn't got it, then they lose interest. And some of the most amazing, great virtuosos didn't get anywhere in Vienna. And some people with much less technique who really got the meaning and emotion of the music they loved. And that's the same in film. I'm very glad that you picked this up, because *craft* to me is a slightly demeaning, a slightly patronizing word. I wouldn't like to call myself an artist, because I think that's kind of pretentious . . . that's just overdoing it. But I'm certainly not just a craftsman. To be a good craftsman in itself is a wonderful thing, but it's not the same.

N: *As you've said, craft is "an instrument." In* From Here to Eternity, *for example, after Maggio [Frank Sinatra] is murdered, Montgomery Clift plays taps, the tears streaming down his face. He has mastered the craft of playing the bugle, but what's more important is that this is the only way he can show his deepest feelings. Isn't this ideally what craft is all about?*
Z: Yes. The thing is . . . I wouldn't want to be misunderstood on the subject. I've enormous respect for craftsmen. To be a good craftsman is a great thing. It's just that it's not quite the exact way to define whatever it is that I do.

Z: I wanted to mention more about camera because I don't think we went into that fully enough. And I'd like to tell you that when I went to school in Paris, to the Technical School of Cinematography [in 1927], there was sort of a new wave, which was called the "Avant Garde." The directors were all very young people: René Clair, Cavalcanti, Epstein, Man Ray, Germaine Dulac, people like that. And they had an expression called *cinéma pur*—"pure cinema"—which meant that the cinema can do things or get things across emotionally that you cannot express in any other way, not with words, not with music—although film is like music, an art which goes directly to the emotions without passing through intellect or through reason. It really addresses itself to the subconscious to a great extent. Anyway, the camera to me is a means of expression rather than simply a technical means of recording. In very many films the camera is used purely to record the action without enhancing it, without taking advantage of any kind of mood it could create. And it's not only lighting, but it's the camera movement and the composition and all sorts of other things.

N: *Are you disagreeing, then, with John Ford, who regards the camera as an "information booth"?*
Z: I totally agree with him, because as he said, "When I move the camera, there's a reason for it." And when you look at a film like *My Darling Clementine*, which is practically all straight set-ups without camera movement, there's one moving shot, which is when the newlyweds Henry Fonda and the girl [Cathy Downs] come around the corner of the barn and start walking. And the camera moves with them and then shows the building, which is about to be raised, with the flag on top of it. And it's a marvelous, emotional moment that is brought about really by the way the camera is handled. So, like any artist, Ford did not establish rigid laws for anything. He used the camera movement when he saw a reason for it, but he didn't move it all over the place. That does not mean that people who move the camera are wrong, because everybody has their own way of telling a story.

N: *Like Max Ophüls, for one.*
Z: Exactly. So what goes for Ford does not have to go for anybody else. But that was what he thought, and that was what I got a lot out of in making pictures like *High Noon*, which had a camera that didn't move all that much, but when it moved—like in the boom shot—there

was a reason for it, and it expressed something. It expressed the loneliness of a man who very probably is going to be killed, with no one else wanting to know anything about helping him.

N: *It's interesting to learn about this particular influence that Ford had on you. Now, what I thought we'd do today is talk about some specific films.*
z: Would it upset you if I had one other thing I wanted to tell you?

N: *No, of course not.*
z: Which has to do with the studios' tampering with films after the films have been made.

N: *Please go ahead.*
z: I can give you one example in my picture *From Here to Eternity*, particularly the scene you were talking about yesterday, the bugle scene. You'll probably be surprised to hear that both Clift and I did not want him [Clift] to cry and that it was an enormous battle between the head of the studio, Harry Cohn, and ourselves. He insisted that Clift should cry. Clift did not feel that he would cry, and I didn't, because Clift and I wanted the audience to cry, not Clift to cry. And by crying, Clift took it away from the audience, even though he was still very strong, but not as strong as we would have wanted to do it. But that was one battle that we lost; we won a great many others.

N: *Were you allowed to film the scene your way, as well?*
z: Yes, we insisted on that. And then there was another battle, because we still said, "Well, the one [take] without the tears is better." But he [Cohn] had the final cut, so there was nothing we could do about it. The other thing in the same sequence was that to my mind it was an homage to John Ford, these other soldiers who are saluting the man who has been killed. And it was a very careful build-up of showing more and more people coming out of the cubby holes and listening. And all of that was cut by the studio to make room for advertising. And also the opening scene was cut from what I wanted, again to condense footage so that they could get more advertising in it. In the original scene, if you remember, the platoon is starting to march across camera,

and then you see a tiny little figure who keeps walking closer and closer. The way this was cut it was covered over with main titles so that you couldn't see it. And originally that was not what it was. It was first the titles, and then you saw the platoon walking, so that the shot ran much longer. Do you follow?

N: *Yes, I do.*

Z: The scene should have been played in the clear to show that this is a man who is a loner and who walks against the stream—because the stream was moving left to right and he was coming closer. This is a subconscious thing for the audience. It interests them. They don't know why, and they needn't know why, but there's something about it that's intriguing. So this should have been a relentless, steady moving forward without a lot of interference from a lot of letters. [Pauses] I gave all of my 16 mm prints to the Academy [of Motion Picture Arts and Sciences] in Hollywood. They have a large amount of material—all my pictures, all my archives, and everything else. And so there is a 16 mm print of *From Here to Eternity*, which is available to anybody who goes there and wants to see it. They let you run it on a Steenbeck.

N: *In other words, this is the director's cut.*

Z: That is the director's cut, yes. That was the original cut. That 16 mm print was taken off the negative after the final preview when the final prints were made for the opening of the film.

N: *Did this sort of tampering happen with any of your other pictures?*

Z: Yes, it happened with *The Day of the Jackal*. They took out about a good twenty minutes. I think they were right to take out fifteen, but they should have left the five others, which were good. But you sit in London, and they are in Hollywood, and what can you do? Besides, they've got thirty lawyers, and you can't fight them.

N: *Tell me about* The Nun's Story. *Did you pretty much get your cut on that film?*

Z: As far as I can remember. Yes.

N: *What about the lunch scene early in the film with Audrey Hepburn and Dean Jagger? A shot from the scene appears in the trailer and also in one of the lobby cards. The scene is even referred to in the opening scene when Jagger says, "Come along, Gaby. I've ordered a table for one o'clock." What took place in the scene, and why was it cut from the finished film?*

z: That scene was cut in my own interest, because I felt it was repetitious and covered an area which you already knew about and also prevented the picture from starting to move. The start was fairly static as it was, and it should not have been burdened with a scene like that, which was meaningless, because it told you nothing new.

N: *How long was the scene? Do you remember?*

z: It must have been about a minute and a half. But that's an awful lot of time, especially at the early start of a picture. It's like a plane starting off: the first two or three hundred yards are always the toughest and the most dangerous, because the audience is trying to grab on to what's going to happen. And if they start getting information they already have, it makes them impatient.

N: *Since we're already talking about* The Nun's Story—*which is my favorite of your films—I'd like to concentrate on it a while longer.*

z: Sure, sure.

N: *In* American Directors *John Fitzpatrick calls it "a transcendent film, comparable more to Bergman or Bresson than to anything in the American cinema" [p. 384]. When preparing the film, did you look at Bresson's* Diary of a Country Priest *or Dreyer's films to see how these European directors had treated the subject of religion, as opposed to how Hollywood had?*

z: Why should I have done that, do you think?

N: *Not that you should have done it. I was just wondering if you had.*

z: Well, I think the last thing I would want to do is to try to imitate anybody . . . to get any help from the outside of that kind. I would prefer to go on my own resources. It's conceivable if I felt helpless or stuck that I might have looked for that kind of help, but thank God I didn't need it. I was very fortunate, and I just did my own work the way I felt.

N: *One thing that strikes me is that, unlike most Hollywood films, it does not treat nuns, priests, or religion sentimentally. That's very much an attitude that you see only in European films.*

Z: Well, that really comes from the enormous amount of preparation that we were able to do, thanks to the Church actually. As you know, I'm not a Catholic, and the Church at first was very careful, because here was the story of a woman who was a professional nun for seventeen years before she left, having discovered that she no longer had the vocation. Secondly, they were worried about what we would do with the implied love story between her and the doctor [Peter Finch]. And it took them a long time to decide that we were okay. Up to that point when we wanted to see a convent, they were always enormously polite, and we would get to see a printing machine or the kitchen, and no more. Later, after there was mutual confidence, they did an enormous amount to let us see what the life of the nuns was like, to the point where the individual actresses who played the main parts—none of whom were Catholics—were allowed to spend about four or five days in a convent. Each one—one person per convent—could then see from the early morning until the Grand Silence at the end of the day what it was like and what happened. They were all in Paris, and I used to make the rounds in a taxi each morning from one convent to another to see how they were doing. All these people—Audrey Hepburn, Edith Evans, Peggy Ashcroft—all these famous actresses were doing it, so that when we finally started to really rehearse, they were already in character, and they knew how a nun walked. There was only one who wouldn't do it for personal reasons, and she was the only one who swung her hips! [*laughs*]

N: *I'm tempted to ask who, but I won't.*

Z: And so all of these people, including Audrey, were all very, very clued in, because they had seen it firsthand.

N: *Even how nuns dismount from a streetcar.*

Z: All of that—the way they held their skirts, how they walked, everything. In fact, at the end Audrey added a touch when she walked out of the convent. She is about to do it [to hold her skirt], and then realizes she no longer has that kind of skirt.

N: *She also leaves the door wide open, which, of course, if she were still a nun, she would have had to close.*

Z: Yes. She also had to leave it open, because we had the camera there [inside the room].

N: *The scenes of convent rituals in the first forty or so minutes depend almost entirely on visuals. How much guidance did you actually get from Robert Anderson's script here? In other words, how detailed was the script? Aren't these scenes an example of where the director is really the creative force?*

Z: Well, I never take credit for work on a script, but in fact I work very intensely on the second draft, and what I do always is ask the writer to write the first draft by himself unless he really wants to talk to me. On the second draft, we work very closely together. And so the thing you refer to is something I saw with my own eyes and then broke down into scenes. And I could say that I had a lot to do with the writing of it, so the script in that sense was in a small way also my script and was there because I felt that that's what it should be.

We were in Rome for this part of the picture, and the people who were in charge of us, as I told you, were the Dominicans. And the man in charge was the head of the liturgy of the Dominican order worldwide. It was in the Mother House, Santa Sabina, and so we saw all the ceremonies of the Dominicans, we saw ceremonies of the Franciscans, and we saw ceremonies of the Augustinians. Then after awhile, the Franciscans would ask us how the Dominicans were doing, and so forth. And they wound up calling me half-brother. [*Laughs*] I'm also probably the only man who ever had the Dominicans and the Jesuits at the same table for dinner!

Well, we were fortunate, because we really did have tremendous, help, [especially] from the Jesuits. There was a man whose name is Father Gardiner. He was the editor of the Jesuit magazine *America* and a professor at Georgetown University, and he was very helpful. I'll give you an idea of the thinking we found within the various communities. There was a scene when the postulants come in and prostrate themselves before [the Mother Superior] Edith Evans, who says in the script, "The life of a nun is a life against nature." That is what was in the book [by Kathryn Hulme]. Our Dominican adviser said, "You mustn't say that. You should say, 'It's a life *above* nature.' " And I said, "Well, I thought that the religious life is a struggle. It didn't mean, then, that you were above nature." And so we went on for a couple of hours to no avail. That evening I saw Father Gardiner, who was in Brussels by chance, and I told him about it, and he said, "Why don't you tell her to say, 'in many ways it's a life against nature'?" And that did it. And that seemed to show the difference between the dogmatic, strict approach of the Dominicans and the very flexible ways of the Jesuits' thinking. It's fascinating to talk with these people. They were very much the top echelon and really brilliant.

N: *Regarding that line, in the film Edith Evans actually says, "In a way it's a life against nature," so she manages a third rewrite and has the final say.*
Z: Yes.

N: *How did you happen to cast Edith Evans and Peggy Ashcroft?*
Z: Because we had a brilliant casting director, Robert Lennard. What normally happens in casting is that the casting director will give you a list of names of actors he thinks might be right for a given part. Let's say he gives you fifteen names. You go through the names, and some of them you know and some you don't. The ones you don't, you say, "Well, can I see a film? Or can I see that actor in the theater, or in a video, or whatever?" And so you then gauge that actor's talent and personality, and gradually in that way, but mainly with the help from a casting director, you arrive at your decision. And Bob Lennard said, "The two people that you should have in this picture are Peggy Ashcroft and Edith Evans." And they both came on interview to the hotel, as a matter of fact, which was rather unheard of. But that's the small amount of merit I had in casting those two ladies. I had more merit in getting other people, who nobody had ever heard of, which was a different thing.

N: *Can you give me some details about how you worked with Audrey Hepburn to shape her role?*
Z: We got together and talked about the character, how it develops, and how it reacts to the other characters. It took many hours of going into lots of details. I always work that way with almost all actors. Then

when we are rehearsing, I always want to see what the actor brings to the part, without telling him what to do. And invariably, if the actor is a talented person with imagination, he has already a well-developed idea about how to bring the part to life.

N: *Audrey Hepburn's face is so expressive that you can read what she's thinking.*

z: It's probably because she and I talked in great detail about what she [Sister Luke] was thinking, but not on the set. We talked about it months before. So she gradually started to live with that and she gradually started to find it in concrete form in the convent when she saw the nuns. And so when we came to shoot, we didn't waste too much time going through explanations. You can work very fast that way.

N: *Because the actor already knows the role.*

z: Yes. But also, you see, working fast is very helpful, because it maintains the energy of the performance. If you do a scene very many times, it may get polished, but it also loses energy. And then you get a very polished scene that is dead. For instance, we shot *From Here to Eternity*, which was very complicated, in seven weeks—forty-two days, which is very fast. And *High Noon* in twenty-eight days, which is four weeks, and very quick. But you have to have the actors prepared to a point where they know exactly when, what, where, etcetera. You know? That explains it for Audrey Hepburn, as well as for any other actor I worked with. Does that give you an idea?

N: *Yes, but it's still hard to imagine, even with thorough preparation and rehearsal, how an actor—in this case, Audrey Hepburn—can summon the kinds of nuances and richness of feeling required right there on the spot.*

z: Yes. Well, that's my job: to create the surroundings where any actor can concentrate. A good actor concentrates tremendously, anyway. . . . And part of the job is to keep actors encouraged, although that's just my own personal feeling. There are other directors who get tremendous performances in all sorts of other ways. I don't say my method is any better than anybody else's, but I happen to work in that way. . . .

N: *How did you work with Walter Thompson, your film editor?*

z: Well, Walter was a marvelous editor. The way I work with editors is that they assemble the film, they cut it as we go. From the first day, we look at the rushes, and then he begins editing the way he sees it. And I never look at it at all until he's got it all completed. By that time the shooting is finished, and he usually has about ten more days to really finish his job. For those ten days I used to go skiing up in the mountains and leave him alone, without pressure. When I came back and he was finished, we'd sit down and look at it. And it would be, let's say, instead of two hours, two-and-a-half hours or whatever. We started then to give it the final shape. And with some editors, it was easier than with others. But Thompson was very good. You were talking about the moving shots when Sister Luke leaves Africa. Well, there was also a moving shot when she first comes to Africa. The first shot is when she sees the station from her point of view. Thompson, a new editor for me—this was the first day on the set—said he wanted to have an establishing shot of the station with the train coming in, and I said, "No way!" because if he had it, he would have used it. And I wanted the shot done from her point of view. That makes a difference. But as Ford said, "If they haven't got it, they can't use it."

N: *The editing style changes in the film. The scenes at the end are much more fragmented than those at the beginning.*

z: Well, yes. Partly because of the tension and the war, and partly because the tempo of life intensifies. It's no longer the idyllic Congo.

N: *The outside world is falling apart, and so is Sister Luke's own private world. And then the last scene returns to the longer rhythm we've seen in the first half of the film. It's a very beautiful and moving conclusion.*

z: Yes.

N: *A scene involving three men trapped in quicksand and rapidly rising water had to be abandoned, because nature refused to cooperate. How and where would it have fit into the film?*

z: Toward the end of the Congo story, but I can't tell you exactly, as I have given my script to the Academy in Los Angeles. My memories of those years (1958–1959) are fading now.

N: *Let's move on to some films we haven't yet talked about.*

Z: Whatever you'd like.

N: *You've said that there was a problem in adapting* A Man for All
Seasons *for the screen. What was this problem?*

Z: Robert Bolt, the author of the play, having delivered the first draft
of the film scenario, said it would be a bad idea to keep the character of
the Common Man because it was, to quote him, "a theatrical device." I
disagreed with him and for several weeks we tried to incorporate the
character in the screenplay, but it stopped the flow of the story; it never
did work and much to my regret we had to finally give up.

N: *Why is Alfred Hayes listed in the credits as one of the writers of* A
Hatful of Rain *[1957]?*

Z: I have no idea. Alfred Hayes was involved on *Teresa* [1951],
because he had written the original book, and I think maybe that he
was hired to write the original script for *A Hatful of Rain*. It quite probably wasn't very good, because I remember that I asked Carl Foreman to
write the script, which he did, but he didn't get credit for it, I don't
think.

N: *Because he was blacklisted.*

Z: Yes.

N: *But didn't Michael Vincente Gazzo write the first draft of the screenplay?*

Z: No, he wrote the dialogue—some of the dialogue—but it was really
Carl Foreman who wrote the script, not Gazzo. Gazzo couldn't write
film scripts, not at that time.

N: *You didn't like using the CinemaScope format in* A Hatful of Rain. *Did
you feel the same way about Todd-AO in* Oklahoma! *[1955]?*

Z: Not really, because it was a different format altogether, and it was
very exciting, because it was something really new [and] experimental.
That was part of why I wanted to do the picture. Normally I wouldn't
touch a musical, because it's not really what I'm good at. But also, the
idea of doing the whole thing on location seemed exciting. To have the

dance and songs out there in Arizona [where the film was shot] was great. Nobody had ever done that before, to my knowledge.

N: *Some critics have said that of all your films* The Sundowners *[1960] looks and feels the most like a John Ford film.*
Z: That's interesting.

N: *What drew you to Jon Cleary's novel?*
Z: I was drawn to it because it showed that there were these three people who had no money and owned nothing except the shirts on their backs and this buggy with the old horse. And nothing could separate them. They were for each other and they were a family, and that was tighter and closer than anything else. And to me that was a celebration of family all the way through, with all the troubles they have. He [Robert Mitchum] doesn't want to settle down, she [Deborah Kerr] wants to settle down, and all that. So that's what it was. Having had a pretty good marriage for fifty-eight years, I'm sort of inclined in that direction, you know. And that's really what I liked about it. That was the whole basic theme, and the book was full of humor and rather sparkling Australian dialogue. I found the Australians at that time [the film was shot in 1959] to be like the Californians in my time thirty years earlier, very simple people with a primitive, very warm sense of humor. You couldn't call them naive, but they were very insular. And they knew what they were about and were very honorable.

N: *Speaking of the Australian dialogue, I like when Deborah Kerr says, "The tucker [food] will be up to scratch!"*
Z: [*Laughs*] Yes, that's the way they talk! It was a happy kind of an occasion [making the picture]. Also, because Peter Ustinov and Robert Mitchum are very funny people, we had a free show every evening for dinner.

N: *Let's talk about Deborah Kerr. The part of Ida Carmody is as much a departure for her as her sultry role was in* From Here to Eternity.
Z: Well, she's just a very, very good actress. She's very adaptable and able to play almost anything.

N: *Isn't this another example of your being able to see a quality in an actor that other people don't seem to have seen?*

Z: I was kind of lucky about that. When the agent brought up Deborah to play the part in *From Here to Eternity*, it was rather startling, because she had never played that kind of a part. She was always an ice cold Queen of England.

N: *In* The Sundowners *she's warm and earthy, and completely believable. The scene in which she watches a wealthy woman on a train powdering her nose is particularly well done.*

Z: That was interesting, you know, because I remember the writer was a lady writer [Isobel Lennart]. That scene had two pages of dialogue in it, which I threw out, because I said it could all be done just with looks. And this writer never forgave me, because her lovely dialogue was thrown out the window, but it would have just killed the scene.

N: *Well, the scene is perfect—we understand exactly what Kerr is feeling.*

Z: That's all you need.

N: *And then Paddy [Robert Mitchum] comes in, and he asks her what's the matter.*

Z: Yes, you then understand that relationship.

N: *Can you comment on the ending? It seems to me that the viewer identifies so strongly with Kerr's desire to have a permanent home that when she gives up the chance—which she does rather suddenly and very good-naturedly—we have mixed feelings. We're happy that the family will stay together, but we're troubled because she may never get her home. Isn't this ending at best bittersweet?*

Z: Well, it's probably true. I must tell you that I can't remember how the book ended, but I remember that I had a very keen feeling of paying tribute to [John] Huston in *The Treasure of the Sierra Madre* when the gold blew away after all these people had gotten killed, and he [Walter Huston] just looked and started to laugh. I wouldn't say I stole it, but something about the human spirit triumphing over what seems to be a disaster made me feel good. It's a very positive thing, and that's what I liked about it.

N: *And so Ida and Paddy laugh, too. They are resilient people.*

z: What good would it be if they got mad and slunk away furiously? It's all negative; it's no good. I think we have too much of that anyway.

N: Five Days One Summer *[1982], your last film to date, seems to me an intensely personal work. How did you come to make it?*

z: That film was based on a sentimental notion I had of showing mountain climbing in the Alps as it used to be in the 1930s when there were considerably fewer people engaging in this sport, which was con- sidered by many to be suicidal and crazy. Having walked in the moun- tains in those days, I had a very strong feeling of wanting to recreate the atmosphere of solitude and silence and majesty which has now dis- appeared from the Alps.

N: *The film deserved a much better reception from the public and critics than it got. In one very intriguing episode, the frozen body of a young bride- groom lost in a climbing accident many years earlier is discovered, and a reunion of sorts takes place with his now aged bride. Is this episode intended as a comment on the triangle involving the three main characters [Sean Connery, Betsy Brantley, and Lambert Wilson]?*

z: The intention was to show the contrast in the lives of two women: the philandering city girl and the old peasant woman who had lost her fiancé in a mountain accident and had never thought of another man for the rest of her life. It is shown in a time-warp of sorts, in the reac- tion of the city girl to seeing the old, old woman confronting her dead bridegroom of sixty years ago, looking miraculously young after being buried in the depths of a glacier. The girl's reaction is, from the point of view of storytelling, the important thing, as it triggers her gradual rejec- tion of her uncle.

N: *I can't believe it, but I see that our time is almost up.*

z: Yes, it's getting there. Let's have one more question, and then we'll finish.

N: *Well, I have so many questions that it's hard to know which one to pick.*

z: [*Laughs*] Go eenie, meenie, minie, moe!

N: *We'll end with* Behold a Pale Horse *[1964]. One motif in the film has to do with the soccer ball that Artiguez [Gregory Peck], the aging guerilla leader, gives Paco, the boy who befriends him. Later, when Artiguez dies, there's a striking subjective shot of the boy kicking the ball in slow motion. What did you have in mind here?*

Z: I had in mind the last impressions of a dying man, what he last sees before he dies. And what he sees is the staircase whirling around and then he sees the ball . . . because at the end of that talk that he and the priest [Omar Sharif] had [about why a priest would help an enemy of Franco and the Church], Peck throws the ball out of a window, and it bounces down the street. That in itself had a symbolic feeling of some kind, which I can't remember, but a lot of people picked that up. And I felt that this is something that stayed in his mind. Why I couldn't tell you. It's not rational.

N: *I thought maybe the ball reminded Artiguez in some way of his own youth. He bought the ball for the boy and at one point he even thinks that the boy hasn't fought—*

Z: —Well, with all due respect, you are trying to rationalize something that is subconscious and totally irrational. Film basically is an irrational thing, and this is an irrational thing—just simply the notion I had because when a man dies, there are some images from his life that accidentally go through his brain. And that's what it was. You'll find as you get older that your mind becomes very selective, that certain cells just die off and the information disappears, and some different brain cells obviously retain other things. I can remember phone numbers of sixty years ago, but I can't remember what I had for dinner last night. It's like that. So it's got nothing to do with rational meanings. . . [It] is not a rational thing at all.

N: *This is a good place to stop. Plus, we're at the end of the tape.*

Z: Probably if we did this for a week, we'd get even more. But you know, unfortunately, that's the way it goes.

N: *Well, we've covered a lot of ground, and there's new material here about your work, too.*

Z: Good. And also there are corrections of some beliefs that have been held that are just not so.

Honoring the Artistry of Fred Zinnemann

VINCENT DEVEAU/1994

On April 29, his birthday, Fred Zinnemann became the first recipient of the John Huston Award for Artists Rights, presented by Steven Spielberg at the International Artists Rights Symposium in Los Angeles. The honoree, to his regret, was not able to attend; at the age of eightyseven, he has been advised for medical reasons that the eleven-hour flight from England might prove too taxing. In his acceptance message read to the assembled audience, Zinnemann expressed his appreciation for the honor bestowed upon him, and charged all present with carrying on the fight in which he has been engaged since the earliest beginnings of the Foundation, and which, in a larger sense, has been a principal theme throughout his long career.

I spoke with Zinnemann at his London home, a townhouse flat in Mayfair a pleasant stroll away from Hyde Park. His handshake is firm and his gaze, for all its warmth, is clear and acute; he has, still, a director's eye, which leaves you feeling that your measure has been well taken.

Age has chiseled rather than diminished him. His bearing is erect, with an almost Old World formality, and although he uses a walking stick these days, it strikes one as a mark of elegance. His speech retains the gentle Viennese accent of the city of his birth, but inflected with English precision and the occasionally surprising American idiom. He speaks softly, an old habit. "There is a very simple trick—to keep your voice so low that people have to strain to hear you," Zinnemann said, explaining his soft-spokeness. "When you came on John Ford's set, it

Originally published in *DGA News* 19, 3 (June–July 1994): 18–24. Reprinted by permission of the Directors Guild of America, Inc.

was like a church. On Mervyn LeRoy's set everybody was cursing everybody else and hollering around, and LeRoy couldn't say more than half a sentence before he had to shout, 'Quiet!' On Ford's set, it was like they were saying Mass."

A quick survey of the room turns up no sign of Hollywood vanity. There is no obvious evidence of his career—no Oscar statuettes, no wall of framed 8 × 10s. The room might as easily belong to a physician—as Zinnemann's own father was, and as he was expected to become—or perhaps a writer or academic, rather than to the man who directed *High Noon, From Here to Eternity, A Man for All Seasons* and *Julia*. The memorabilia is personal rather than professional, and the mantelpiece is given over to a display of family photographs, many of his son Tim.

Zinnemann—three-time Academy Award-winner, and recipient of the DGA's D. W. Griffith Award for distinguished achievement in motion picture direction—has earned the admiration and respect of filmmakers many times over, both for his body of work and for the integrity with which he has conducted his career. Most recently, he has been instrumental in the battle for legal recognition of artists' moral rights, both as a founding member and as honorary trustee of the Artists Rights Foundation. I began by asking how he came to be involved with the issue.

"A friend of mine, George Stevens, Jr., told me about the threat of colorization, which was then in its infancy," he related. "Nobody took it very seriously at the time. Then I saw the first films that came out, which were absolutely horrifying. There were several friends—David Lean was one, and two or three others—and all of us agreed that this should not be done, that the vision of the picture maker should be preserved as it was in the original. It was that simple.

"It was, to begin with, a very informal kind of arrangement," he continued. "Gradually it coalesced, and the moving spirit was [Artists Rights Foundation President] Elliot Silverstein, who was very devoted, very dedicated, and who began to organize a response. It so happened that I knew Congressman Robert Mrazek, who became enormously interested, and who made great efforts in the House of Representatives."

It was around this time that Zinnemann wrote to then-President Ronald Reagan, warning him of "another kind of 'High Noon' . . . a cultural crime against a genuine American art form and against our national heritage." Any sort of helpful or positive response, however, would be a long time coming. "There was a slow build-up, suffering primarily from the lack of public opinion, which we tried to counteract by sending various very well-known actors and directors to lobby for us," Zinnemann explained. It was a series of individual efforts, and by degrees, it grew and grew."

From those individual efforts, the Artists Rights Foundation was established in 1990 with the dual purpose of educating the public about the threat to its motion picture heritage, and to institute a legal fund which would carry the fight for moral rights into the courts. Zinnemann made it very clear that he is not himself a campaigner. The practical credit for the Foundation and its efforts he accorded entirely to Silverstein and to those who carry out the daily work. As a guiding muse, however, the reputation which Zinnemann has acquired over a lifetime of standing his ground and resolutely going his own way would be difficult to improve upon.

Zinnemann arrived in Hollywood in 1929, having abandoned early dreams of becoming a musician ("I had hardly any talent at all," he confessed), and declining to follow his family's tradition into medicine. Following a period of study at the then newly opened Technical School of Cinema in Paris, he had spent a year working as an assistant cameraman in Berlin—where he crossed paths with a number of other struggling newcomers, among them Billy Wilder and Marlene Dietrich. An early mentor was the documentary filmmaker Robert Flaherty, whose formative influence was later to have an enormous impact upon Zinnemann's directing method.

His work in Mexico with photographer and producer Paul Strand on *The Wave* (1935) brought Zinnemann to the attention of Jack Chertok in the MGM Shorts Department, where he served a three-year apprenticeship. "It was a very, very helpful experience," he recalled. "I was making short subjects and learning how to develop economy—not in terms of money but in terms of storytelling. How do you tell a story in ten minutes? That came in very helpful in pictures like *High Noon,* where each scene was a sequence of its own, so to speak, and you had to know in your own head how it was going to come together. It was a marvelous training for that kind of thing." Even that apprenticeship was not to go unrecognized, as Zinnemann won his first Oscar for one of those short subjects, *That Mothers Might Live,* in 1938.

Overall, the director had much good to say for the studio system and the men who ran it. "Far be it from me to knock the studio system, because there was a lot going for it. First of all, you had four or five years—if you were lucky—to develop, to learn your craft, in terms of production values, photography, editing and everything else."

Recalling his dealings with the studio bosses—Harry Cohn of Columbia in particular—Zinnemann praised them for their "gambler's instinct. . . . That's what showmanship was. You didn't need computers to figure it out. You did it by the seat of your pants. . . . Show business at some point changed into 'the entertainment industry,' that in itself tells you the difference," he stressed. "The people in charge of show business were showmen who loved the medium, who loved movies. Today it's an industry cold-bloodedly devoted to making a profit; quality is secondary, and there's no love lost. It's without passion, and the picture maker is usually treated as a necessary evil."

For all the merits he saw in it, the studio system and Zinnemann came inevitably to a parting of the ways. "After *The Seventh Cross* (1944), I had what seemed a very bright future for a while, but there were some arguments," he recalled. "I was contractually forced to do two films I didn't want to do, and thank God they have disappeared, more or less." The two films—*Little Mister Jim* (1946) and *My Brother Talks to Horses* (1947)—were vehicles for MGM child star Butch Jenkins, and following that experience, said Zinnemann, "I just didn't want to do any more." After the almost unheard of insubordination of refusing several scripts in a row, he accepted a suspension, and when he still didn't cave in to front office pressure, "Metro was quite happy to loan me out for a year to go to Europe to make a picture about war orphans, which was *The Search* (1948)."

The *Search*, which received an Oscar nomination for the then-virtually unknown Montgomery Clift, won several important awards, including Oscars for non-pro child actor Ivan Jandl, as well as for writers Richard Schweizer and David Wechsler, and a special award from the United Nations. It also marked the beginning of a relationship with producer Stanley Kramer which was to continue through *The Men* (1950) and *High Noon* (1952), and allowed Zinnemann to establish a position as a director independent of the studios.

"It was necessary," he said, explaining his need for independence. "I was not cut out to be a company man. I'm not very good at taking orders when it comes to being told what to do and how to do it. You were told, 'This is the script, it starts shooting in three weeks, the sets are already going up, Susie Glotz is going to play the lead. Any other questions?' After a while, that was it for me. When my contract expired, I just didn't want to renew it."

Returning to his European roots had another effect on Zinnemann's thinking: "It opened my eyes. In Hollywood, people were still dedicated to the happy ending, to illusion and to the caricature of life." In Europe meanwhile, it was "the era of neorealism, people like Rossellini and DeSica. When I came back to Hollywood, I felt I wasn't quite the same as I had been when I left, while generally people continued to do fake stories with fake endings."

Zinnemann continued, "I was predisposed to that sort of semi-documentary work because in my formative years I was very much under the influence of Robert Flaherty, who was, after all, the grandfather of documentaries. Working with real people in real surroundings—it was something that appealed to me enormously, and I felt that making a picture in the place where it was supposed to be happening—in that *very* place—gave you an extra something that you could not possibly get in a studio." While the semi-documentary style of *The Search* would persist to a greater or lesser degree through *The Men* (1950) and *Teresa* (1951), its impact would diminish over time while still continuing to flavor all Zinnemann's work to follow. What would not diminish, however, was the filmmaker's independent cast of mind. The productions of *High Noon* and *From Here to Eternity* (1953) were not without controversy. McCarthy-era suspicions about Carl Foreman's script for *High Noon*, as well as more commercial considerations revolving around Floyd Crosby's unusually stark black and white photography, dogged that production. *From Here to Eternity*, which earned Zinnemann his first feature direction Oscar, seems a tame enough exercise today, although in its time it took an unprecedentedly critical look at the U.S. Army— when looking critically at such institutions was still fraught with peril.

Zinnemann was on the front lines again when the Communist witch-hunts of the fifties made their mark upon the Screen Directors Guild. A virtual "palace coup" had taken palce on the National Board: a loyalty oath had been written into the Guild's by-laws during the temporary absence of Guild President Joseph Mankiewicz, against whom a recall was then mounted.

"The dangerous thing in the Guild at that time was that practically the entire Board, with very few exceptions, was definitely pro-McCarthy, and Mankiewicz wasn't," Zinnemann recalled. "The first 'invitation' to sign the oath came by mail from the Board, saying they have decided that this should be done to demonstrate our loyalty to the United States. It was pretty forceful. At that time, there must have been about five hundred-odd members in the entire Guild, and most of them signed.

"As I remember it, there were about fourteen who did not sign and said so, and then about fifty who didn't sign without declaring. I was one of those," he continued. "After a few weeks, there was another, more urgent letter from the Board, saying that they were ashamed that there were still some members who didn't sign, and that the office would be open on Saturday so there was no excuse for not signing, and would I come and sign, please. Again, I didn't answer. So the third thing was, not exactly a reign of terror, but they started sending people on motorcycles, late in the evening, coming with this piece of paper, saying 'sign here.'"

Zinnemann continued, "At that point, John Huston called a meeting—there were five or six of us—and he said, 'Boys, the fat's on the fire.' I remember those words. He said that the only way to beat this was to ask for a general meeting, but in order to do this you had to be a member 'in good standing.' As the McCarthy group on the National Board had already said that unless you signed [the loyalty oath] you were not a member in good standing, we all signed. We found twenty-five people who were willing to do this."

The next step was to petition for a general meeting, and it was one's signature on *that* document which put one's career in jeopardy. "At that time—especially for the younger directors who were not established—there weren't any direct threats, but there were heavy hints that your career was on the line," he added. "You sign this and you've had it. In spite of this, we signed. . . . [Billy Wilder] did, and Fritz Lang, a number of people, Huston of course. And so I signed."

The general membership meeting which followed represented a turning point for the Guild and one of its finest hours. Zinnemann was in

New York and therefore not able to be present at the meeting, but recalled, "The clinch came when [Cecil B.] DeMille pulled out a piece of paper and said that this was signed 'by Mr. *Vy*ler, Mr. *Vi*lder, Mr. Zinne*mann*' and the membership started to boo him. [John] Ford got up—he who was very, very right-wing—and said to DeMille, 'I don't like you, I don't like what you're saying, I don't like what you stand for.' Then he moved that the Board should resign. I don't recall who seconded it, but there was a vote, and the Board was forced out. Then they called a new Board, of which I had the honor of being a member."

The years which followed took Zinnemann ever more frequently back to Europe, and he began to feel a bit out of touch with America during the sixties, having been largely absent during the years of the civil rights struggle and the Vietnam War. "From a certain point onward, I found myself making pictures that were based in England because of the Eady Plan [a trade protectionist measure which taxed movie tickets to help finance British film production] and other reasons . . .," he said. "Gradually, as things go on, one takes root. At the same time, California recedes because the old people die off. . . . You miss the crucial experiences, you lose contact." His problems with the Hollywood studios were not yet over, however.

After three years preparing to film the screen adaptation of André Malraux's *Man's Fate*, MGM pulled the plug just three days before the start of principal photography, and—as Zinnemann had been engaged on a 'handshake' rather than a contract—Metro proposed to stick him with a $1.7 million pre-production bill as well. "That was when a hand-shake stopped being a handshake," he said. "Before that, if you shook hands you had a deal. After that, you could shake as many hands as you wanted, but the lawyers took over."

It was a watershed moment for the old Hollywood, and Zinnemann still laments its passing. "When you hear the old time anecdotes you can see how far we've come," he added. "John Ford, before he started shooting *The Informer*, asked the producer, Cliff Reid, to come down and be introduced to the crew. Ford called for quiet and said to the crew, 'I want you to meet our producer, because this is the last time you're going to see him. . . .' Or the one about Ford's grandson who wanted to get into the movies, and asked his grandfather how he should go about it. Ford said, 'Well you should start at the absolute bottom and work your way up. I suggest that you become a producer.' "

Problems or not, the flow of great pictures continued unabated: *The Nun's Story, The Sundowners, Behold a Pale Horse, A Man for All Seasons* (which earned Zinnemann his second directing Oscar), *The Day of the Jackal, Julia* and *Five Days One Summer*. While audiences and his fellow filmmakers continued to find Zinnemann's work praiseworthy, a sour note was sounded by proponents of the auteur theory, whose view was rather more skeptical. Zinnemann's films lacked a personal stamp, it was claimed by critic Andrew Sarris, who found that his directorial style was without the "commitment" which marks the true auteur. The implication was that Zinnemann was somehow less than fully the author of his own work, and the charge, years later, still rankles.

"It is his privilege to dislike my films, but his reasons seem ridiculous and not worth discussing," Zinnemann said. Personally, he considers Sarris' authorship theories "an obsolete joke, first perpetrated by the young Frenchmen of the 'New Wave'—a joke they quickly got tired of." He views the question of authorship quite simply: "The writer is the author of the script. The cinematographer is the author of the photography. The composer is the author of the music, and the producer is the author of the production. They, and many others, are *associate authors*, but the director is the only person who knows how to blend all these works into the final shape and style of the movie he envisions. He is the principal author.

"*The Grapes of Wrath* is a novel by John Steinbeck," the director continued. "The screenplay is the work of Nunnally Johnson, but the film is by John Ford. Without making comparisons of value, we can take an opera, *Figaro*, for instance. It is not the librettist da Ponte's *Figaro*, it is not the dramatist Beaumarchais' *Figaro*—it is Mozart's *Figaro*. Opera is driven by music, as film is driven by moving images. The parallel is obvious. Whether or not the work was or was not done 'for hire' has nothing to do with it."

Given the range of Zinnemann's films—everything from the near-documentary realism of *The Search* to the musical comedy of *Oklahoma!*—the application of the auteurist criterion of an unvarying formal style is ludicrously inappropriate. If Zinnemann chose to place his direction at the service of his material, he did so consciously and with a clear motive. "The director's job is to lift the material from the written page and to put life into it," he explained.

It is also worth remembering that the auteur theory was originally concerned as much with thematic consistency as with *mise-en-scene*. A thread of such consistency—'individual action compelled by con-science' might be one way of characterizing it—is plainly evident throughout the director's best films. This is clearest, perhaps in *High Noon*, the picture which Zinnemann feels is the most likely to endure. "*High Noon* doesn't seem to have any particular age, because the theme is permanent—it's close to human nature which never changes," he said. "You can be scared stiff and still try to do what you think is right."

Before our conversation concluded, Zinnemann recalled a final anec-dote, related to him by Flaherty in the days when both spent a winter together cooling their heels in the bar of Berlin's Adlon Hotel, waiting for the agreement which would take them to Russia to film a documen-tary. "It was to be about a tribe in central Asia; the Kirghiz or the Tadzhiks, one of those," he explained. "The Russians wanted to show how primitive it all was until the Soviets came and created a paradise, and Bob wanted to do a picture about a culture that was being gradu-ally submerged by something alien. Opposite thinking. They were at it for about six months and never got anyplace.

"By sitting with him, though, drinking beer and listening to the man, I learned more than I had any right to learn—what it means to compromise and not to compromise and how far do you go? My whole attitude toward making films, trying to create something that is more than a piece of pretentious junk—I learned that from Flaherty. He just wouldn't budge. I think he only made six pictures in his whole life, because of that."

Zinnemann continued: "Bob told me a story then which I've never forgotten. It's about a young merchant marine sailor on shore leave in Bombay. He comes into a temple and there's a Hindu monk there who takes him around and shows him a statue of Buddha. In front of the statue is a lamp, and the monk explains with great awe and respect that it has not gone out in five hundred years. With that, the young sailor wets his thumb, pinches the flame and says, 'Well, it's out now.'"

For Zinnemann, the story is important for its tragedy as much as for its humor, and it is not difficult to understand why. One has only to think of the ease with which it is today possible to colorize, time-compress and pan-and-scan his life's work, and that of all other great filmmakers of the past. "Well, it's out now," they will tell us. And when they do, what will we answer?

Several days following our meeting, Zinnemann and I spoke again on the telephone and ended up talking about the church scene in *High Noon*—Carl Foreman's "stroke of genius" as he puts it—which so brilliantly parodies the rationalizations of democracies facing inconvenient crises. From that, our conversation took a wider turn. Bosnia had been much in the news again, and Zinnemann spoke of the parallels he saw between that situation and the indifferent international response to the Spanish Civil War almost sixty years earlier, as well as that still-earlier crisis in Sarajevo which set the world to war, and which is still within the range of his memory.

As I listened, an impression I had formed during our interview came back to me: the man's mind seems driven by a kind of intellectual, even moral compass, which compels him to pursue the sense of things, to locate a pattern, a balance, and if possible, some notion of right. That moral compass, which informed the best of his work, is undiminished by the years. It still seeks true north, and it draws Fred Zinnemann along with it.

A Past Master of His Craft: An Interview with Fred Zinnemann

BRIAN NEVE/1996

CINEASTE: *Would you say that Robert Flaherty influenced your style?*

FRED ZINNEMANN: Flaherty wrote me a letter of introduction in 1931, and as a result I got a job at Goldwyn. He influenced me in every possible way, not only technically, but also in what I learnt from him by being his assistant, his whole spirit of being his own man, of being independent of the general spirit of Hollywood, to the point where he didn't worry about working there. That's probably why he made only five or six pictures in his life. But he influenced me in his whole way of approaching the documentary, which he really initiated with films like *Nanook of the North.*

I learned from Flaherty to be rather uncompromising and to defend what I wanted to say and not let someone else mix it up. He had the true feeling of a documentary director—he took life as it was. This influenced me enormously, because I found myself almost subconsciously following his style in films like *High Noon, The Men,* and particularly in parts of *The Search,* which I made after the war. This was not really a documentary, but it was in a style beyond the then fashionable approach, which involved a mandatory happy end and marriage as the solution to all problems.

So, first of all, my choice of subjects pushed me in that direction, and time and again there was a documentary kind of treatment—in *The Nun's Story, The Day of the Jackal,* and even *Julia.* I've always tried to base my films as closely as I could on the reality. Even in casting, if a woman

Originally published in *Cineaste* 23, 1 (1997): 15–19. Reprinted by permission of *Cineaste*.

was described, as in *The Search,* as a Czech, then I really wanted a Czech, not a Hungarian. There are so many subtle, subliminal things that go into making a film, that I have to insist on getting that particular kind of nuance from the authentic person, rather than getting an approximate idea of "virtual Czech" or "virtual Hungarian."

CINEASTE: *I like The Search very much, especially the scene with the children in the ambulance who suddenly fear that they are being taken to their deaths and flee. Was that influenced by Italian neorealism?*
ZINNEMANN: It was influenced by Flaherty, not by the new realism in Italy. At that time nobody had even heard of Auschwitz, and very few people knew anything about what had happened in Europe. It was a new approach to picture making at that time. I think we were the first Hollywood company that went out on a distant location, because before then the factory process was much more strictly observed by the studios. They wanted to have complete control of making a film, so they avoided working on distant locations where conditions were not controllable by the studio. They would send out a second unit to photograph a background, bring the background material back, put it on a screen, and then play the action in front of it. So you could get a Chinese rice field with a non-Chinese actress playing Chinese. We could have made *The Search* in Hollywood, obviously, just as we had to make *The Seventh Cross* in Hollywood, because it was wartime, and one could not go to Europe. But I learned all of that when I directed my first picture, *The Wave,* which was commissioned by the Mexican government.

The Wave was, in a sense, also a legacy from Flaherty, because it involved people who were friends of his, like Paul Strand. The director, Henwar Rodakiewicz, had a conflicting commitment and asked me to take over. The government at that time was liberal. It was just before the great Mexican President, Cardenas, who was himself an Indian. So what we were doing was following the government's socialist program. I was at that time still politically naive, but what I found exciting was that it dealt with oppression. I had always thought that human rights were above property rights, but I belonged to no party. I was never politically organized.

CINEASTE: *Were you happy with how* The Wave *turned out?*

ZINNEMANN: I was surprised that anybody wanted to look at it, because at the time I had no idea whether I communicated with anyone. It was an experiment. So I was very pleased that there was that much attention given to it. But I was not pleased with the ending. The earlier part was better, and I was very happy to be working with fisher-men who were not actors but fishermen. It makes a hell of a difference, even down to the way they tie their knots. This, to me, is the essence of picture making.

CINEASTE: *Were you impressed at this time with Soviet filmmaking, and especially with Eisenstein?*

ZINNEMANN: Enormously, yes. Eisenstein, and *Potemkin* especially, was important in my development, not only because of the concept of montage in shaping the film but also because it was about oppression.

CINEASTE: *What aspects of* The Seventh Cross *appealed to you?*

ZINNEMANN: *The Seventh Cross* was bought by MGM and written by Helen Deutsch, who was a good writer. It was at a time when we were fighting Germany, and every German in the eyes of the American peo-ple was a monster. The book and the film made the point that even in Germany there were people who had the courage to go their own way and stand up against what was happening. I thought that was very important and exciting. Of course, the fact that Spencer Tracy was playing the lead made it even more exciting, because I was still really an apprentice.

You see, I go by the old idea of guilds, in which there are three stages. You are first an apprentice, then you become a journeyman, and, if you are still in one piece, you eventually become what they call a master. This sounds pretentious, but it is a fact that at that stage you have more or less mastered your craft. I do not particularly like to think about myself, but having done so, I feel that my apprenticeship was over after I had completed *The Search*. When I returned to America, I made *Act of Violence*, and I felt that I already knew what I was doing, rather than going by instinct, as before. From *Act of Violence* until the end of *The Men*, I was a journeyman, and after that, for better or worse, I felt that I had arrived at where I was the person in charge. Maybe those early days were really the best, who knows?

CINEASTE: Act of Violence *has a distinctive look to it, with the location shooting and high-contrast lighting.*

ZINNEMANN: The cameraman, Bob Surtees, was a brilliant photographer and an old friend I had known in Germany. We got to know each other in 1928 when we were both assistant cameramen and used the same dark room. Bob was a very creative, marvelous photographer, one of the best that I worked with. I've had good luck working with wonderful cameramen. Another interesting thing—you don't mind if I ramble?—is that directors normally like to work with one cameraman and stay with him, like John Ford and Gregg Toland, and so on. People have asked why I did not do this. The answer is that I cast cameramen like casting actors, in terms of the style of the picture and what I hope the photography will bring to it.

If you make a picture like *High Noon*, and you want to make it feel like the world felt in the days of the Civil War in America, that kind of gritty, dusty feeling, you had to get a cameraman who knew how to handle that, like Floyd Crosby, who was not the greatest man to photograph a woman. But if, on the other hand, you had a picture like *Julia*, where you had two actresses who were close to forty, or just beyond forty, and who had occasionally to look like teenagers, you had to have a very good portrait photographer, and that was Douglas Slocombe. He was a wonderful cameraman, and great at this kind of romantic, warm feeling. Had *Julia* been photographed by Floyd Crosby, it would have looked totally different. So I changed cameramen as the material dictated.

CINEASTE: *What was the political atmosphere like in the late forties? Was it a great shock when the House Un-American Activities Committee began its hearings on Hollywood in 1947?*

ZINNEMANN: One could not say that it was a shock in terms of surprise, because everything was moving towards that. There was increasing tension, brought about by the fear in America of the communist conspiracy, the notion that there were lots of communists under the bed. In fact, there were quite a few crypto-people, most of them not even card-carrying members. But there was a tremendous suspicion, and the American people in normal times are not suspicious. The McCarthy thing did not come as a surprise, but it developed gradually as his

speeches and radio appearances went on. People became politically suspicious, and they were helped by many of the politically far-right. This
whole phobia about communism went on and on, and is still going on,
although now they are called liberals. It was not a shock. It was something that one saw coming, just as one had a sense that war would be
coming in 1939, when all the sabre-rattling started to become reality.

CINEASTE: *In Kenneth L. Geist's biography of Joseph Mankiewicz, the*
director H. C. Potter is quoted as saying that you were blacklisted for a time
during this period, when your name was used by a group that was declared
subversive, and that you appeared before an American Legion Committee to
clear yourself. Can you confirm this?
ZINNEMANN: Yes, probably. I'd forgotten that, but it may have been
true. Many filmmakers were attacked at the time of the famous
Directors Guild meeting. This was the meeting when John Ford, who
was far right, turned it around and really destroyed De Mille and his
whole group. At the height of the McCarthy business, C. B. De Mille
and his group, who were the Board of the Screen Directors Guild,
decided that all members should take a mandatory loyalty oath. First of
all, they said that any new members should take it, but then they
decided that everyone should, as an expression of loyalty to the country. Well, a lot of people felt that they did not need to demonstrate
their loyalty and objected to the idea of being coerced into doing it.

There were then about six hundred members in the Guild, no more
than that. Of the six hundred there were fourteen who said "No," who
were, I believe, communists. There were about five hundred who voted
"Yes," and about fifty-five or fifty-six who did not say anything one way
or the other, including myself. So we then received a polite reminder
from the Board, a letter saying that such and such a day would be the
deadline, and please be sure to sign, which I did not do. Next there was
a cable, which sounded very tough and very officious. Again I did not
respond, and at that point scare tactics started, with people on motorcycles coming late in the evening, asking for the signature.

There were about ten to fifteen of us, with John Huston being very
prominent at that point. The only thing we could do was to call for a
general meeting at which the whole membership would have to vote—
a referendum in other words. But, in order to be able to call a general

meeting, you had to be a member in "good standing," and what the
C. B. De Mille people had done before was to pass a bylaw saying that
in order to be in good standing you had to sign the loyalty oath. So, in
the end, twenty-five of us signed this thing, and the well-known
general meeting did take place.

It was a good feeling to stand up against these people, but of course
you didn't know quite what was going to happen. It was all right for
the very successful, who were sure of their jobs, but for the young directors, without a strong record in the industry, it was more difficult,
because there was a blacklist. There was a bush telegraph among the
studios as to what color you were—black or red or white. And it is possible that, in connection with that, I went to the Legion, probably to
sign that oath, without which the meeting could not have been held.

It is curious that I don't remember it. I am sure that it must be true.
Certainly there was never any question of being asked about names—
ever. In order to call a general assembly of the Guild, the rule was that
there had to be twenty-five directors in good standing who could ask
for such a meeting. And in order to be in good standing you had to sign
the loyalty oath. Which is why Potter and I and a number of others
signed it, not for any other reason.

CINEASTE: *Did the political pressures during that period make it more difficult to make more realistic or socially conscious films?*
ZINNEMANN: Generally, very much so, but in my case, no. I don't
know how it happened, but I know that, at the time that we made *From
Here to Eternity*, the Army was absolutely sacred because of Korea and
the victory in WWII. So one would have thought that to make a picture
like *From Here to Eternity*, which was critical of what went on inside the
Army, and what it did to individuals, would not be possible. Except that
Harry Cohn, who was a very bright showman and someone with a
sense of what the public would accept, bought the book. Everyone
thought he was crazy. It took him two years to get a reasonably good
script—in fact, it was a very good script—by Daniel Taradash. Then I
was asked if I would like to direct it, which at the time was amazing,
because it was the prize assignment of the year at Columbia.

I was not aware of any overt difficulties, except certain things that the
Army could not live with. They did not want us to show what happened

in the stockade where Sinatra got beaten up, which was fine with all of us, because you saw the result of it, with Sinatra coming out and falling dead. The other thing was that the real villain of the piece, the captain (Deborah Kerr's husband) was promoted to the rank of Major in the book. The Army insisted that he get his comeuppance, by either resigning or being court-martialed. So this was the one, unavoidable compromise, but it was worth making, because I could not have made the picture without professional soldiers who knew how to march and drill. If you had a lot of extras slouching around, it would have been nonsense. We also had the free run of the entire location in Hawaii where the thing really had happened. But those were the only difficulties we had with the Army. We had some problems with the Church, but they were very understanding about the beach scene, which was very startling at the time.

CINEASTE: *When you made* High Noon, *were you aware that Carl Foreman intended it as a comment on Hollywood in the McCarthy period.*

ZINNEMANN: No. I read much later that Carl saw the piece as an allegory of his own personal experience. I did not think of it in political terms. To me the film was about conscience and degrees of compromise. Most people, when they encounter such a situation, will rationalize their way out of it, they will always have a reason why they can't help. This was the main theme, from the coward, to the man who really would help if he were not the only supporter, as against the drunk and the kid, who are so out of touch with reality that they want to help the Marshal.

CINEASTE: *How did you regard people such as Elia Kazan and Clifford Odets, who named names?*

ZINNEMANN: It is hard for me to say, given that I was not in the same situation. I hope I would not have done it, you know, and I hated it. Maybe they were weak, but you can't judge other people unless you really know what's behind it. Eventually you find out that they were victims of something that may have happened when they were small. The whole question of why somebody is a criminal is difficult. You can't just sit and read headlines in a newspaper and be sanctimonious about it. So I don't approve of Kazan or Odets at all. In Kazan's case the

important thing is that he made some fantastic pictures and con-
tributed a tremendous amount, in theater and film. At the same time I
admire Arthur Miller very much, given the way he behaved at the time.

CINEASTE: *Was the crane shot, towards the end of* High Noon, *unusual at the time?*

ZINNEMANN: It's curious, but although it is a shot that technically
would have been possible before, I don't remember ever having seen
anyone do it that way. I wanted to express the fact that this man was
totally abandoned by everybody, and all doors were closed to him. He
had nowhere to go, except to face the music. In the last analysis, I am a
visual person. I'm not very good with words, but I think I can express
things visually that somehow connect with the audience, because
audiences seem to remember them for a long time.

The crane we used was an enormous monster which could be rented
for the day. Across the street George Stevens was shooting *Shane,* I
think. We borrowed it from him for a day and it needed ten people to
move it. Now you could do it with a zoom shot, but it would not be the
same thing.

CINEASTE: *After the success of* From Here to Eternity, *why did you choose
to make* Oklahoma!?

ZINNEMANN: Because I was offered it and I found it fascinating to try a
new medium, this huge screen. And to work with Rodgers and
Hammerstein was a great pleasure. Looking back, I'm surprised that
they picked me—it had no logic. They did it because I was a "hot"
director at the time. *Oklahoma!* had come out on the stage during the
war, at a time when everyone was very depressed. Suddenly there was
this gorgeous music, and this upbeat feeling about the world being a
great place, and everyone took courage from it. So everyone had a good
deal of affection for this particular musical, even though it has no story,
other than that of who gets to take the girl to the dance.

CINEASTE: *Was it true that you hired a ballet troupe for* The Nun's Story,
for the scenes with the postulants in the convent?

ZINNEMANN: Yes, it is true. We needed good faces for the close-ups of
the nuns. In terms of the movement of the various ceremonies we needed

people who could respond to rhythm, not just extras who would shamble around. So we did get twenty or thirty people from the ballet, who were perhaps a shade too precise. You know, looking back, I feel critical of the fact that it all looked kind of glamorous. Originally I had wanted to shoot all of them in black and white and have only the tropical scenes in color so that the austerity of Europe would contrast with the bursting tropical fertility of the African scenes. But I got beaten down on that—win some and lose some. At least one could argue with the studio boss about it.

CINEASTE: *I was struck by the last scene, where Audrey Hepburn finally leaves the convent. The camera stays inside, so there is less of a sense of triumph than had the camera been outside.*

ZINNEMANN: We had a very good composer, Franz Waxman, who wrote good music for the ending. I did not want to use it, and he was very upset, so we finally had a meeting with the head of the studio, Jack Warner, who was a good showman. He said that every Warner Bros. picture had music at the end. I said that if the music was upbeat, would it not suggest that Warners was congratulating the nun on leaving the convent? So we won. I always wanted her to go out in total silence, with just one bell at the end when she goes round the corner.

CINEASTE: *In the recently published* Sight and Sound *dossier, a letter from you to Harry Cohn was published, in which you suggested that the release of* From Here to Eternity *be delayed in Europe. Can you explain why you wrote that letter?*

ZINNEMANN: You would not believe it, but at the time Americans were loved in Western Europe and were looked upon as the saviors who had gotten rid of the Nazis. I felt that showing a picture like *From Here to Eternity* in Europe would damage this euphoria. Cohn didn't understand the point, and, in any case, the film was making a lot of money for Columbia.

CINEASTE: *What impressed you about Emeric Pressburger's novel, which became* Behold a Pale Horse?

ZINNEMANN: Thinking about it now, I cannot tell you. The film didn't really come together, and the book didn't either. At the time I could not find any other projects that I wanted to do. But I was not very happy about it, except that some of it was interesting to make. I met a lot of people who had been resisting Franco, many anarchists who had left Spain and were living just across the border so they would not lose the smells of their country. Many of them were in Perpignan. It was interesting, but it did not really feel right except in a few spots. There were one or two of my pictures that were like that.

CINEASTE: *How did you plan the visual style of* A Man for All Seasons, *and the very strong sense of the distance between Chelsea and Hampton Court?*

ZINNEMANN: There were a few technical problems. There was no place we knew of that had the right kind of house and a river, all in one. There is a scene where the king jumps from his boat into tidal mud, so it had to be a tidal river. You had to find a time when the tide was out and the sun was at the same time in the best position for photography. That gave us one or two days a year. All the river mouths in England are full of modern shipping and modern architecture, so we had to find part of a river that looked pristine.

Somebody discovered a place near Southampton where the owner had the rights to the river. So we rented the location, which was usually a kind of garage for yachts, for five or six weeks. At the end of that river we built a wall, and then we built the same kind of wall in Oxfordshire, where there was an Abbey we could use. So in the film the king would climb the wall in Hampshire and descend from it in Oxfordshire. It is nice to have a challenge like that.

CINEASTE: *How do you remember working with Orson Welles?*

ZINNEMANN: It was totally unpredictable, but a lot of fun. He had a great sense of humor. We made Cardinal Wolsey's room very small on purpose, so you felt that there was not any oxygen in it, that he took it all up. The art director, John Box, did a brilliant job. Everything was in red, the Cardinal and the walls, and he sat there, big and fat, looking totally unlike Wolsey, but it really didn't matter. In addition, for research, having the Holbein portraits of all these people was terrific. We did not use all the details, because it would have cost too much, and anyway people would have been watching the costumes instead of the actors, which is a great danger in costume pictures.

CINEASTE: *When you made* The Day of the Jackal, *how important was the characterization of the Jackal? Was it important, for example, that he be an upper-class Englishman?*

ZINNEMANN: Not all that much. The important thing was to have a man who can become invisible. There was nothing special about him, so he could be one of the crowd. If you had a big star, it would have ruined the whole movie. This was part of a long battle I had with the studio, who wanted a star. There were several stars who wanted to be in it, but then the film would have become a vehicle for the star, and that was not the story. Edward Fox happened to be sort of upper class, but that was not mandatory.

CINEASTE: *When Robert Shaw, as King Henry VIII, emerges out of the sun in* A Man for All Seasons, *was that an image you planned?*

ZINNEMANN: It was the idea of Robert Bolt, the writer, who always wanted to get the feeling of him coming out of the sun. There is one thing that maybe should be said about the director. Basically he takes the script and brings it to life. It comes up in arguments about who is the author of a film. David Lean said that the author of the script is the writer, the author of the photography is the cameraman, and the author of the editing is the editor. They are all associate authors, but the principal author is the person who puts it together and makes it come to life. No one else can do that, certainly not the producer. Legislation which suggests that the person who finances a film is the author is ridiculous. Billy Wilder is the author of his films, not Paramount!

There are going to be many battles fought over this, because the financial boys want to be the authors. In America they managed to remove the clause stipulating moral rights of authorship from the Berne Treaty. It is a very important question and, unless it is resolved eventually in favor of the director, you will always have films like *"Terminator 26,"* without imagination, and with a colossal amount of money wasted, with half of it not visible on the screen. We were trained to try and see the biggest part of the dollar on the screen. Some of these old Hollywood proverbs were pretty wise. Another was that you meet the same people going down as you met going up. It was a great life, I must say, and it is now totally different. There is a tremendous amount of talent, but there is a very worrying lack of what I have to call soul, because I cannot call it anything else.

CINEASTE: *Did you have disagreements with Hellman over* Julia?
ZINNEMANN: Lillian Hellman wrote a book called *Pentimento,* with chapters which supposedly dealt with her life. In a short story called "Julia," she wrote about a woman she knew and had helped in Germany, which was not true. Lillian Hellman in her mind owned half the Spanish Civil War, while Hemingway owned the other half. She would portray herself in situations that were not true. An extremely talented, brilliant writer, but she was a phony character, I'm sorry to say. My relations with her were very guarded and ended in pure hatred.

CINEASTE: *Are you pessimistic or optimistic about the cinema as you have known it this century?*
ZINNEMANN: I would like to be optimistic, because we have brilliant directors and writers and actors, but I tend to be pessimistic. We have enormous powers of persuasion, and we are role models for the rest of the world, but we no longer have a positive attitude towards life. Until that is changed, I think it is not going to be good.

My own credo is borrowed from the words of William Faulkner, who expressed them in his speech when accepting the Nobel Prize in 1951, and which have stuck in my memory ever since: "I believe that the human spirit will prevail forever. It is our privilege to help it endure by lifting people's hearts, by reminding them of Courage and Honor and Hope and Pride and Compassion and Pity and Sacrifice, which have been the glory of their past."

INDEX

CONVERSATIONS WITH FILMMAKERS SERIES
PETER BRUNETTE, GENERAL EDITOR

The collected interviews with notable modern directors, including

Robert Aldrich • Pedro Almodóvar • Robert Altman • Theo Angelopolous •
Bernardo Bertolucci • Jane Campion • Frank Capra • Charlie Chaplin •
Francis Ford Coppola • George Cukor • Brian De Palma • Clint Eastwood •
John Ford • Terry Gilliam • Jean-Luc Godard • Peter Greenaway • Alfred
Hitchcock • John Huston • Jim Jarmusch • Elia Kazan • Stanley Kubrick •
Fritz Lang • Spike Lee • Mike Leigh • George Lucas • Michael Powell •
Martin Ritt • Carlos Saura • John Sayles • Martin Scorsese • Steven
Soderbergh • Steven Spielberg • George Stevens • Oliver Stone • Quentin
Tarantino • Lars von Trier • Orson Welles • Billy Wilder • Zhang Yimou

.